DECISIONS FOR DEFENSE

STUDIES IN DEFENSE POLICY

DECISIONS FOR DEFENSE: PROSPECTS FOR A NEW ORDER

William W. Kaufmann
John D. Steinbruner

THE BROOKINGS INSTITUTION
Washington, D.C.

ℬ THE BROOKINGS INSTITUTION

The Brookings Institution is an independent organization devoted to nonpartisan research, education, and publication in economics, government, foreign policy, and the social sciences generally. Its principal purposes are to aid in the development of sound public policies and to promote public understanding of issues of national importance.

The Institution was founded on December 8, 1927, to merge the activities of the Institute for Government Research, founded in 1916, the Institute of Economics, founded in 1922, and the Robert Brookings Graduate School of Economics and Government, founded in 1924.

The Board of Trustees is responsible for the general administration of the Institution, while the immediate direction of the policies, program, and staff is vested in the President, assisted by an advisory committee of the officers and staff. The by-laws of the Institution state: "It is the function of the Trustees to make possible the conduct of scientific research, and publication, under the most favorable conditions, and to safeguard the independence of the research staff in the pursuit of their studies and in the publication of the results of such studies. It is not a part of their function to determine, control, or influence the conduct of particular investigations or the conclusions reached."

The President bears final responsibility for the decision to publish a manuscript as a Brookings book. In reaching his judgment on the competence, accuracy, and objectivity of each study, the President is advised by the director of the appropriate research program and weighs the views of a panel of expert outside readers who report to him in confidence on the quality of the work. Publication of a work signifies that it is deemed a competent treatment worthy of public consideration but does not imply endorsement of conclusions or recommendations.

The Institution maintains its position of neutrality on issues of public policy in order to safeguard the intellectual freedom of the staff. Hence interpretations or conclusions in Brookings publications should be understood to be solely those of the authors and should not be attributed to the Institution, to its trustees, officers, or other staff members, or to the organizations that support its research.

FOREWORD

SINCE the autumn of 1989, changes of epic scale have transformed Eastern Europe and the Soviet Union. Germany is united. The Warsaw Pact has dissolved. The authoritarian rule of Communist parties has ended in Poland, Czechoslovakia, and Hungary and now in the Soviet Union itself. Reform politicians throughout the region are committed to developing constitutional democracies and market economies. Their purposes are threatened far more by internal ethnic tensions and economic disruption than by the traditional prospect of imperial conquest.

A new era in international politics has been heralded by previously unthinkable actions. The Soviet Union gave political and diplomatic support to the United States and coalition forces in expelling Iraq from Kuwait, and has worked collaboratively to resolve other regional disputes. Large reductions of conventional and nuclear weapons deployments have been mandated by treaty. Unilateral reductions in national forces seem likely to exceed even these historic mandates.

In this study, William W. Kaufmann and John D. Steinbruner review the defense establishment the United States has inherited from the cold war. They then consider the impact of the changes in Eastern Europe on the defense budget and on the assumptions underlying it. They conclude that the latest plan proposed by Secretary of Defense Richard B. Cheney still retains many of the assumptions of the cold war, and that the United States can safely reduce its defense budgets and forces well below the levels sought by the Pentagon.

Kaufmann and Steinbruner propose two defense budget scenarios that differ sharply from the Cheney plan. The first challenges the Cheney assumptions about the future international environment, postulates a traditional system of collective security periodically organized to deal after the fact with specific crises, and takes advantage of certain efficiencies that together could reduce defense budget authority by 47 percent between 1990 and 2001, compared with the Cheney plan. The second option goes beyond the first to propose a more permanent system of cooperative security. This system reduces uncertainty sufficiently to permit a cut in the defense budget of at least 53 percent over the same period, compared with the Cheney plan. Cumulative savings over ten years could range from $300 billion to $400 billion in 1992 dollars.

Kaufmann and Steinbruner argue that both the collective and the cooperative security budgets would allow for the maintenance of a survivable and controllable nuclear deterrent. Both could provide sufficient non-nuclear forces to duplicate the most critical deployments of Desert Storm, even though the authors do not foresee such a demanding contingency during the next ten years. Finally, they assert that the two budgets could afford high readiness and sustainability, rapid overseas deployment, and continued modernization through the upgrading of current weapons systems and a selective procurement of proven next-generation capabilities.

William Kaufmann is a professor emeritus at the Massachusetts Institute of Technology and a senior fellow at Brookings. He holds the Sydney Stein, Jr., Chair in International Security in the Brookings Foreign Policy Studies program. John Steinbruner is director of the Brookings Foreign Policy Studies program. They are grateful to Patrick Bogenberger for his comments on the manuscript. Nancy D. Davidson edited the manuscript, and Vernon L. Kelley verified its factual content. Members of the staff of the Foreign Policy Studies program provided word processing, and Charlotte B. Brady and Susanne Lane provided administrative assistance. Susan L. Woollen prepared the manuscript for typesetting.

Brookings is grateful for funding provided by the John D. and Catherine T. MacArthur Foundation, the Carnegie Corporation of New York, and the W. Alton Jones Foundation.

The views expressed in the study are those of the authors and should not be ascribed to persons or organizations whose assistance is acknowledged, or to the trustees, officers, or other staff members of the Brookings Institution.

BRUCE K. MAC LAURY
President

September 1991
Washington, D.C.

To Sydney Stein, Jr.

CONTENTS

TABLES

CHAPTER ONE

INTRODUCTION

As EARLY as 1985, members of Congress began to question the rapid growth in U.S. budget authority and spending for defense that had been launched by the Reagan administration in 1981. By 1989, as communist regimes collapsed in Czechoslovakia, East Germany, Hungary, and Poland, many voices were being raised to suggest that the cold war had ended, national security policy needed a drastic revision, and the time had come to cut the defense budget in half during the next ten years.

Since 1989 dramatic events have continued to occupy the international stage. Yet national defense spending remains close to $300 billion. Budget authority for defense has declined by almost 22 percent in constant dollars since 1985, but spending has fallen by only 3.8 percent (table 1-1). Secretary of Defense Richard B. Cheney has argued that peace itself is the only real peace dividend. Perhaps the maintenance of a new world order will turn out to be as expensive as the conduct of the cold war. Nevertheless, it seems even more obvious than it was in 1989 that the competition of the past forty-five years is over and that major changes in defense policy and programs are in order.

It may be argued with considerable merit that the United States is able to spend whatever is necessary to maintain the basic conditions of national security. Indeed, the history of the last fifty years, including World War II, has shown that to be the case (table 1-2). But it is also the case that the United States, like the Soviet Union, has paid a large price—on the order of $12 trillion (in 1992 dollars)—for national defense since the "unconditional" surrender of Japan.[1] This tax on the national income has contributed to a national debt of more than $3 trillion, a current deficit rapidly approaching more than $300 billion, and the

1

Table 1-1. Budget Authority and Outlays for National Defense, Fiscal Years 1985–91[a]
Billions of 1992 dollars

Year	Budget authority	Outlays
1985	376.2	320.5
1986	359.5	338.5
1987	346.1	339.4
1988	339.0	338.5
1989	334.2	339.8
1990	327.6	324.7
1991	293.8	308.2

Source: Defense Budget Project, *Analysis of the FY 1992–93 Defense Budget Request* (Washington, February 7, 1991), tables 3, 4.

a. The budget for national defense includes funds for the Department of Defense, the military applications of atomic energy (carried in the budget of the Department of Energy), the strategic stockpile, and the selective service system. The functional classification of national defense is 050. The military activities of the Department of Defense are a subfunction of national defense and are classified as 051. The civil activities of the department are not included in either category.

assessment by President Bush that citizens have "the will but not the wallet" to support or expand other programs. Perhaps so, but those same citizens are entitled to ask whether, as circumstances continue to change, the price of defense should not fall by a considerable amount.

After some delay, the administration has come to recognize the changes that are taking place in the international environment. The president himself has proclaimed a new world order, even though it promises to be neither very new nor very orderly. Secretary Cheney has accepted the idea of modest real reductions in the defense budget. And Congress has agreed with the executive branch on the Budget Enforcement Act of 1990, which could reduce spending for national defense, in real terms, by another 22 percent or more from fiscal years 1990 through 1996. This agreement—combined with the ejection of Iraq from Kuwait, a considerable economic recession, and presidential elections in the offing—has left Congress almost content to live with the Pentagon's budget totals for fiscal 1992 and 1993, even though they were intended as ceilings rather than floors. So far, key congressional committees appear likely to do no more than a slight reordering to the Defense Department's priorities during the next two years.

Perhaps that is as much as can be hoped for or expected of the budgetary process in fiscal 1992 and 1993. The rules of the game will change, however, for fiscal 1994 and 1995. Congress will have some latitude within overall ceilings to transfer resources among the major funding categories. National defense no doubt will thereby become a

Table 1-2. Defense Department Outlays as a Percent of Gross National Product, Selected Fiscal Years, 1945–90

Year	Percent of GNP
1945	38.0
1950	4.4
1955	9.1
1960	8.2
1965	6.8
1970	7.8
1975	5.6
1980	5.0
1985	6.2
1990	5.4

Sources: U.S. Bureau of the Census, *Historical Statistics of the United States, Colonial Times to 1970*, pts. 1 and 2 (1975), pp. 230, 1115–16; and *Department of Defense Annual Report, Fiscal Year 1992*, p. 111, table A-3.

major target for further reductions, particularly as domestic issues rise to the top of the congressional agenda.

In anticipation of these opportunities, it is not too early to raise six questions and try to answer them. First, what is the defense inheritance from which changes will inevitably be made, and what are the assumptions underlying this vast legacy? Second, how and to what extent are these assumptions being undermined by the changes that have already occurred in the world? Third, what was the initial response of Congress and the administration to the new environment, and how did the Iraqi invasion of Kuwait alter this response? Fourth, what is the "long-range" plan of the Defense Department as proposed in February 1991, and what are the assumptions underlying it? Fifth, what issues arise from these assumptions and plans? And sixth, although the national defense budgets appear to be relatively fixed for fiscal 1992 and 1993, what can be said about the options over the next ten years? In short, where do we go from here?

Endnote

1. William W. Kaufmann, *Glasnost, Perestroika, and U.S. Defense Spending* (Brookings, 1990), table 1. The numbers in the table have been converted into 1992 dollars, based on Defense Department estimates of inflation.

CHAPTER TWO

THE INHERITANCE

THE U.S. ROLE in the cold war was shaped by four events that occurred during or shortly after the end of World War II: the concentration of the United States on the destruction of Hitler and the reconstruction of Europe; the arrival of Soviet armed forces in the heart of central Europe; the detonation by the United States of the first nuclear weapon, along with the deployment of long-range heavy bombers; and the doctrine of containment as articulated by George F. Kennan in his long telegram of 1946 from Moscow to the State Department.[1]

The situation in Europe led to the direct confrontation between U.S. and Soviet forces, the Berlin blockade, the formation of the North Atlantic Treaty Organization (NATO) and the Warsaw Pact, and periodic tests of will between the two sides. The atomic bomb and the B-29, followed by thermonuclear weapons and more powerful heavy bombers and intercontinental and submarine-launched ballistic missiles (ICBMs and SLBMs), all contributed to the establishment and growth of the U.S. strategic nuclear forces and to a somewhat comparable arsenal in the hands of the Kremlin. They also created another source of rivalry between the two superpowers. Containment was originally an abstraction, but after the Soviet occupation of Eastern Europe and what was seen as the Soviet-inspired invasion of South Korea by North Korea, it became one of the foundations for a major U.S. military capability. Not only did it consolidate the view that U.S. interests were worldwide; it also reinforced the case for meeting the USSR at every turn and preventing the Kremlin from encroaching on those interests, either by deterrence or by a forward defense (fortified with nuclear weapons) if necessary.

From this view of containment flowed multilateral and bilateral mutual security treaties, executive agreements, military assistance pacts, base rights, and less formal pledges of support. All of them could have been (and often were) interpreted as potential military commitments on the part of the United States.

Force Planning

It is one thing to talk about interests and commitments. It is quite another to translate them into military capabilities and budgets. The literature on defense frequently contains discussions about the global interests and commitments of the United States, followed by leaps to a "requirement" for specific U.S. forces—without any explanatory link.[2] Equally often, debates will arise over the issue of whether commitments exceed capabilities or vice versa, again without any explanation of how the two relate. The assumption appears to be that wherever a commitment exists there must be the forces necessary to fulfill it.

Fortunately for the national purse, U.S. force planning has not worked that way. For thirty years or more, planners have had to focus on specific threats and possible attacks (or contingencies). They have then had to define specific military objectives, specific allied contributions, and the specific U.S. military inputs needed to give a desired probability that the objectives could be achieved at an acceptable cost. In addition, planners have had to decide how many of these contingencies might arise more or less simultaneously, and for how many of them, and in what fashion, the United States and its allies should prepare a response. A variety of capabilities, both nuclear and non-nuclear, have complicated these decisions and made the costs of deterrence and defense more onerous than in previous history.[3]

The problem of deciding how much of these capabilities is enough has also plagued the planners. Clearly they have considered it essential to include the contingencies that would threaten such vital areas of U.S. security as Western Europe, northeast Asia, the Persian Gulf, and of course the United States itself, even though there was only a small probability that enemies could attack all these areas simultaneously. But what about other less critical contingencies that might have arisen at the same time or quite separately? Should the planners have included the forces to deal with these as well?

Obviously issues of cost and risk are involved here, although they have received little systematic attention. As a consequence, most presidents, without quite knowing what they were doing, have been willing to bet that if the forces to cover the most threatening contingencies could be acquired and maintained at acceptable cost, they could divert enough of these forces to handle the lesser cases without undue risk. In sum, presidents have wagered that, despite the plethora of U.S. interests and commitments, they would have to fulfill only a limited number of them at any one time. They have also gambled that, at least for force planning purposes, the Pentagon could identify the most critical contingencies by the location and magnitude of specific threats (such as where large Soviet forces were deployed), and by the importance of the threatened area—such as Western Europe or the United States itself.

This approach to force planning may not seem very sophisticated as the necessary link among interests, commitments, and military capabilities. But nothing better has come along during the last thirty years. Moreover, for better or worse, the approach has had a great deal to do with shaping the cold war forces of the United States as well as their modifications that the Pentagon is now proposing.

The Fiscal 1990 Budget

It is noteworthy in this connection that, although the Defense Department presents its budget requests to Congress in several different formats, none of them shows either the major forces and their annual costs (table 2-1) or their allocation by planning contingency (table 2-2). Admittedly, methodological problems arise in making such presentations because it is difficult to impute indirect costs to particular forces, and the forces themselves are more fungible than the planning contingencies may suggest. It is possible, nonetheless, to calculate these allocations to a first approximation for any particular fiscal year, including 1990. The defense budget for that year is the last in what may be thought of as the long cold war series.

These informal presentations call attention to a number of issues that do not ordinarily play much of a role in debates about defense. A great deal of attention goes to the modernization, operation, and

Table 2-1. Budget Authority for Major U.S. Forces, Fiscal Year 1990
Billions of 1992 dollars

Type of force	Budget authority
Strategic nuclear forces	48.2
Tactical nuclear forces	2.4
Non-nuclear forces	
Army divisions	
Active duty	70.3
Reserve	9.3
Marine Corps	
Active-duty divisions	6.6
Active-duty air wings	9.0
Reserve division	0.6
Reserve air wing	0.6
Air Force fighter wings	
Active duty	48.5
Reserve	5.4
Navy	
Carrier battle groups	53.5
Amphibious capabilities	8.3
Antisubmarine warfare forces	21.2
Airlift	10.9
Sealift	2.5
National intelligence and communications	19.2
Total (051)	316.5

Sources: *Department of Defense Annual Report, Fiscal Year 1992*, app. C, pp. 75–77; and authors' estimates. See Appendix for further information.

maintenance of the forces. Much less attention is given to their size, composition, and missions. It has become the conventional wisdom that 50 percent of the U.S. defense budget is allocated to the defense of Europe, but little is said about the forces that produce that calculation. And virtually nothing is known publicly about the cost of providing U.S. forces for the defense of Korea or the resources devoted to the destruction of hard targets in the Soviet Union. Yet these data are at least as important as the price of a B-2 stealth bomber or an M-1A2 Abrams tank.

The Basis for the Strategic Nuclear Forces

The cost of the U.S. nuclear forces in 1990—including strategic and theater-based nuclear capabilities as well as weapons costs, most of which are carried in the budget of the Energy Department—amounted

Table 2-2. Budget Authority Allocated to U.S. Force Planning Contingencies, Fiscal Year 1990
Billions of 1992 dollars

Force planning contingency	Budget authority
Strategic nuclear deterrence	48.2
Tactical nuclear deterrence	2.4
Non-nuclear defense of:	
North Norway	16.7
Central Europe	90.3
Mediterranean	7.6
Atlantic sea lanes	21.7
Middle East/Persian Gulf	64.5
South Korea	19.0
Pacific sea lanes	14.7
Alaska	1.4
Panama and Caribbean	3.2
Continental United States	7.6
National intelligence and communications	19.2
Total (051)	316.5

Sources: Table 2-1; and authors' estimates.

to less than 20 percent of the national defense budget in fiscal 1990. The strategic forces accounted for more than 95 percent of that total. They consisted of 1,828 launchers and 12,058 nuclear warheads, depending on how each delivery vehicle was loaded with weapons (table 2-3).

Several factors are largely responsible for the size of these forces. They are (1) a substantial list of targets in the Soviet Union, consisting of strategic and general-purpose forces, communication nodes and command centers, air defenses, power sources, transportation systems, and well over 1,000 separate urban-industrial aiming points; (2) the demand that, on average, the survivable force have the capability to destroy 80 percent of the targets, with particular emphasis on hard strategic targets, whether occupied or empty; (3) the assumption that the Soviets would strike first against U.S. forces on a day-to-day alert with only fifteen minutes' warning; and (4) the further assumption that only about 25 percent of the ICBMs, 30 percent of the bombers, and 60 percent of the SLBMs would survive the attack to retaliate and launch weapons after having penetrated enemy defenses (which would inflict losses almost exclusively on the bombers).[4] It is hardly surprising that, given such a conservative and demanding scenario, it was

Table 2-3. Capabilities of U.S. Strategic Retaliatory Forces, Fiscal Year 1990

Item	Launchers	Warhead inventory[a]	Alert warheads[b]	Alert, survivable warheads[c]	Deliverable warheads[d]
B-1B	90	2,160	648	648	415
B-52G	58	696	209	209	134
B-52H	96	1,728	518	518	332
Minuteman II	450	450	405	101	81
Minuteman III	500	1,500	1,350	338	270
MX	50	500	450	113	90
Poseidon C-3	176	1,760	871	871	697
Poseidon C-4	192	1,536	829	829	664
Trident C-4	216	1,728	1,011	1,011	809
Total	1,828	12,058	6,291	4,638	3,492

Sources: *Department of Defense Annual Report, Fiscal Year 1992*, p. 115; and authors' estimates.
a. Based on authors' assumptions about force loadings.
b. As a percent of warhead inventory: bombers, 30 percent; ICBMs, 90 percent; Poseidon C-3s, 49.5 percent; Poseidon C-4s, 54 percent; Trident C-4s, 58.5 percent.
c. As a percent of alert warheads: bombers and SLBMs, 100 percent; ICBMs, 25 percent.
d. As a percent of alert, survivable warheads: bombers, 64 percent; ICBMs and SLBMs, 80 percent.

assumed that the large inventory of nuclear weapons would shrink to approximately 3,500 deliverable weapons, or fewer than necessary to cover the entire target list with the high degree of confidence demanded by strategic planners.

Because of this alleged deficiency, it is also hardly surprising that a demand should have existed for larger and more survivable forces. Nor should it astonish anyone that the Air Force struggled to modernize its bomber and ICBM components while the Navy continued to replace its aging Poseidons with the larger Trident ballistic missile submarines. After all, the doctrine of the triad, promulgated when ICBMs and SLBMs were not particularly reliable, still remained in effect. According to this doctrine, bombers, ICBMs, and SLBMs would serve not only to confuse and dilute opposing defenses, but also to insure against the possibility that an enemy might develop effective countermeasures to one or two of the triad's three legs.

Most presidents since the mid-1960s have endorsed the triad and the growth of the strategic nuclear weapons in general as the list of targets in the Soviet Union has expanded. All presidents since 1961 have eventually accepted the need to maintain a range of options so that, in the event of a nuclear exchange, they could withhold portions of the offensive forces. Such options require an even greater emphasis on the survivability and endurance of the launchers, although the choice of option would depend on the scope and weight of a Soviet attack. Much less of a consensus has emerged on the desirability of exploring the prospects for efficient antiballistic missile and antisatellite defenses, and there has been even less agreement on the need to strive for an early deployment of either system and to abrogate or modify the Antiballistic Missile Treaty of 1972. And many arguments have arisen about the meaning and merits of strategic nuclear superiority over the Soviet Union, what constitutes the conditions of deterrence, and the kind of goals the United States should set for its strategic nuclear forces in the unlikely event that deterrence should fail. However, none of the positions taken in these debates has exercised much influence on the size and composition of the strategic nuclear forces or their costs.

Indeed, it became almost axiomatic that no serious reduction in forces or launchers would prove feasible with an adversary as hostile as the USSR without verifiable agreements aimed at achieving comparable cuts on both sides. In principle, changes in the basic planning scenario could have been made to increase the survivability of U.S. bombers and SLBMs. And the list of targets could have been cut. It could have included fewer silos, since so many of them would be empty under the standard scenario of a Soviet surprise attack. There could also have been fewer launch control centers or nuclear storage sites on the list if all the silos were going to be attacked, and fewer urban-industrial targets held hostage since the relatively prompt deaths from more limited strikes would still have been in the millions. For some targets, precision-guided munitions might even have been substituted for nuclear weapons.

In these circumstances, U.S. forces could have been reduced without a treaty, and some degree of modernization could have been deferred since concerns about force survivability and defense penetration would have diminished. But the dictates of minimal risk, along with the expectation that the strategic competition would continue and that the USSR might gain an advantage (if it had not already done so), made any such exercises in restraint at best hypothetical. The dominating principle was that although the probability of a failure of deterrence was low, the consequences of such a failure would be catastrophic. Therefore heavy insurance was worth buying, whatever the policy's effects on the strategic competition.

The Basis for the Tactical Nuclear Forces

Flexibility about the size and composition of the theater-based nuclear forces proved to be greater. At or near its peak, the U.S. stockpile for these forces apparently contained more than 10,000 weapons for use against targets on land, at sea, in the air, and under water.[5] The total stockpile may not have declined significantly since 1983, but the number of nuclear weapons deployed in Europe (mostly Germany) had dropped from 7,000 to approximately half that number by 1990. Only air-delivered weapons may remain there in the near future. However, the decline has resulted more from Germany's growing resistance to the continued presence of short-range nuclear delivery systems on its soil and congressional refusal to modernize key portions of the stockpile than from any change in the Pentagon's view about the role of nuclear weapons in the defense of Western Europe.

That role, intended to enhance the deterrence or defeat of an attack on the members of NATO, was based on two assumptions. The first was that the Warsaw Pact, dominated by the Soviet Union, would hold a substantial superiority over NATO in non-nuclear forces. The second was that NATO, by a first use of nuclear weapons against tactical targets, including concentrations of enemy troops, would be able to nullify the advantages of the Warsaw Pact.

Despite the development of a larger nuclear capability by the Soviet Union and a number of analyses suggesting that the Warsaw Pact's non-nuclear superiority was more apparent than real, NATO continued to insist that its threat of a tactical use of nuclear weapons remained essential to the security of its members, and that its leaders would somehow manage to be the first to authorize their employment. As these leaders saw it, the prospect of escalating a conflict to a full-scale exchange between the United States and the Soviet Union added a dimension to deterrence that non-nuclear forces could never achieve by themselves. As one might imagine, it was considered to be in the poorest taste even to whisper that precisely because this prospect was so terrifying, NATO's threat, especially in a severe crisis, would not be truly credible. What was more, because the land-based nuclear forces in Europe were so vulnerable, the Soviet Union might consider the threat as a standing invitation to initiate a preemptive strike of its own.

The Basis for the Non-nuclear Forces

This peculiar attitude did not go unmatched. One of the more interesting aspects of the cold war is that the Pentagon consistently argued that allied forces could not withstand a full-scale non-nuclear attack by the "Red hordes" (whether Soviet or Chinese or both) without an early resort to nuclear weapons, yet it managed to sustain support for large, increasingly powerful, and costly non-nuclear forces at the same time. The basis for these forces was what became known as the 2½-war strategy, which turned into the 1½-war strategy during the Nixon administration. This so-called strategy more or less remained in place for twenty years, despite talk during the Reagan administration of a worldwide strategy and frequent allusions to attacks on Soviet vulnerabilities by such unlikely means as carrier battle groups and Marine amphibious forces.

These strategy labels are misleading. For planning purposes, a worldwide strategy still requires the identification of specific theaters of operation. The defense of Western Europe alone could actually involve three separate land theaters—north Norway, the central region of Europe (that is, Germany), and southeastern Europe (Greece and Turkey)—as well as three sea lines of communication requiring protection by major naval forces, many of which would be American. A standard assumption, still in effect as late as 1990, was that either preceding or immediately following a widespread European conflict, a Soviet invasion of Iran would occur, involving still another theater of land operations and a long sea line of communications requiring naval protection. Planners also postulated that under these conditions U.S. forces in South Korea, Alaska, and Panama would require reinforcement and that a protected sea line of communications would have to be established in the Pacific as well. Furthermore, at least modest forces would remain in the continental United States (CONUS) for training, maintenance, and overhaul and, if necessary, to intervene in case of Cuban-incited troubles in the Caribbean and Central America. In the event of such widespread hostilities, the strategic nuclear forces would presumably go to a generated alert, with as many as 50 percent of the bombers and 80 percent of the SLBMs ready to launch.

Despite such complexity, one aspect of the planning stands out: two of the largest contingencies and most of the justification for the size and composition of the U.S. non-nuclear forces arose from actual concentrations of Soviet forces and from U.S. assumptions about the hostility and aggressiveness of the Kremlin, which were fortified by the Soviet invasion of Afghanistan. To note these assumptions is not to argue that when the fiscal 1990 budget was presented the planners should have changed their conservative estimates of the potential threats or of the U.S. inputs required to support a forward defense in Europe, southwest Asia, or Korea.

In north Norway, the danger existed that a substantial Soviet force could not only subjugate a NATO ally but also complicate seriously the defense of the sea lanes between Europe and America. It made sense, therefore, to pre-position U.S. matériel in Norway and plan on deploying a division and an air wing there. Unfortunately, however, the Pentagon assigned the mission to the Marine Corps, which gave the Navy the basis for justifying three carrier battle groups in support of the operation, thus making the cost of the contingency higher than it needed to be (table 2-2).

In central Europe, the main threat came from the concentration of forces from the Warsaw Pact located in East Germany, Czechoslovakia, Poland, and the three western military districts of the USSR. Much concern existed in NATO over the possibility of a short-warning attack by as many as 90 Warsaw Pact divisions, of which 59 would be Soviet, despite their widespread lack of combat readiness and the rapidly growing power and skill of the U.S. tactical air forces. In addition, there was always the possibility that over a longer period of mobilization and deployment the Warsaw Pact could mass up to 111 divisions against the central region of NATO. For the United States, even counting the contributions of allies, these contingencies meant the continued deployment of six division equivalents and eight fighter wings in the region as well as twelve more active-duty and National Guard divisions and more than fifteen fighter wings held in the CONUS for reinforcement.

To execute such large-scale deployments would have meant the rapid movement of well over a million tons of equipment and supplies, the deployment of more than half of the U.S. ground and tactical air forces, and the use of the large stocks of matériel pre-positioned in Europe and aboard ships in nearby waters. Consequently, heavy emphasis was placed on expanding the fleet of military airlift aircraft and wide-bodied planes drawn from the Civil Reserve Air Fleet. Fast sealift received much less attention, although the Carter administration did acquire eight commercial ships with a top speed of thirty-three knots (the SL-7s of Desert Shield notoriety) and began their conversion to military use.

In the circumstances, it is easy to see why the central European contingency alone accounted for 29 percent of the 1990 defense budget (table 2-2). That figure, moreover, did not include the costs of defending north Norway or the Atlantic sea lanes, which would have concentrated primarily on the threat from Soviet attack submarines and could have required the Navy to protect more than five large convoys a month. Nor was the defense of NATO's southern flank a part of these costs. Yet here too the planners assumed a large threat from the Warsaw Pact. Hungary, Romania, and Bulgaria, backed by Soviet forces in Hungary and in the southern military districts of the USSR, were considered capable of launching a major offensive against Greece and Turkey. Depending on the circumstances, the United States would, at a minimum, have supported its allies with aircraft from the 6th Fleet in the Mediterranean; and if other conditions permitted, a Marine Corps division and air wing might also have been committed to the theater.

In sum, the U.S. contribution to the non-nuclear defense of Norway, the central region of Europe, the Atlantic sea lanes, and NATO's southern flank came to approximately $136 billion, or more than 40 percent of the defense budget for fiscal 1990 (table 2-2). If the cost of covering the strategic and tactical nuclear threats to Europe is included, the U.S. allocation of resources to the defense of Europe amounted to nearly 50 percent of the budget authority for national defense.

In addition, until well into 1990, the presence of five Soviet divisions in Afghanistan and another nineteen opposite Iran was considered the main threat to the states of the Persian Gulf and the basis for determining the size of the forces the United States should have available for deployment to the area. Planners estimated that more than six divisions and the equivalent of nine fighter wings would have to be on hand to halt a Soviet attack. And since no U.S. forces were stationed in the region, it was deemed necessary to deploy three carrier battle groups, together with at least one Marine amphibious force (supported by maritime pre-positioning ships in the Indian Ocean), to provide an early response to such an attack. Although the threat shifted from the USSR to Iran by the time of the fiscal 1991 budget, the forces included in the Persian Gulf contingency package remained the same as before and cost as much as $64.5 billion a year (table 2-2).

None of these costs, it is worth noting, includes the substantial funds ($19.2 billion) allocated to national intelligence and communications. However, it seems reasonable to suppose that well over half of that was related to watching and analyzing the Soviet nuclear and non-nuclear forces.

The only contingency of some consequence for planning purposes that could be considered relatively free of Soviet influence and support was the threat of a surprise attack by North Korea on South Korea. Although some planners and policymakers had argued for years that South Korea could readily provide for its own defense, the United States continued to deploy an infantry division and more than a wing of fighter aircraft in the republic. Furthermore, conditions permitting, another two divisions and the equivalent of nearly three more fighter wings would have been deployed in a crisis. Beyond that, the Navy would have needed the ships and submarines to protect the sea lanes to Korea and Japan in the event that either China or the USSR attempted to sever them. The price for this support amounted to $33.7 billion a year.

Another $12.2 billion was allocated for more mundane purposes. Garrisons in Panama and Alaska were to be maintained and strengthened. At least four carrier battle groups were to be in home waters for overhaul and training. Some of them, along with several divisions and fighter wings, could have formed a Caribbean task force. Alternatively, they could have been used to reinforce one of the main theaters. To a degree, even these reserves reflected a suspicion that the Soviet Union might cause trouble across the Bering Strait and in Central America.

The Costs of Cold War Security

In retrospect, it is difficult to calculate how much of a return in security the United States obtained from its forty-five-year investment of approximately $12 trillion (in 1992 dollars) in national defense. Without much greater knowledge, primarily of Soviet intentions and plans, it remains uncertain whether a smaller share of the gross national product allocated to the armed forces would have yielded equal returns in deterrence and defense. What does seem clear, however, is that none of the commitments went unfulfilled as a result of the planning approach adopted and the forces it helped to produce. Despite alarms about bomber gaps, missile gaps, and windows of vulnerability, the U.S. strategic forces ensured that the probability of a nuclear exchange remained low, even at the peak of the Cuban missile crisis. Non-nuclear conflicts did occur, but none was lost for lack of U.S. military capabilities. Perhaps this was because at no time in those forty-five years did more than one military challenge to alleged U.S. interests arise at any given time. As a consequence, adequate forces were always available for the unexpected contingency, whether in Vietnam, Grenada, or Panama. In these respects, the planning and the strategic concept appear to have passed the test of time. The cost was high, and it may have been greater than necessary, especially during the 1980s. But despite repeated alarms from the Pentagon, the planners and their policymakers won the bet that the risks of disaster were acceptable and even quite low.

Endnotes

1. Dean Acheson, *Present at the Creation: My Years in the State Department* (Norton, 1969), p. 151.
2. For a recent example, see General Carl E. Vuono, "Desert Storm and the Future of Conventional Forces," *Foreign Affairs*, vol. 70 (Spring 1991), p. 57. General Vuono also makes a standard, parochial, and unsupported allegation that the "Army of the mid-1990s will be a perilously small land force for a nation with the United States' superpower responsibilities." See Walter S. Mossberg, "Even the Scaled-Down Military Machine Planned for '95 Would Leave the U.S. a Still-Potent Force," *Wall Street Journal*, March 14, 1991, p. A20.
3. The term *non-nuclear* is used throughout the text because many weapons now available are no longer conventional.
4. Donald R. Cotter, "Peacetime Operations: Safety and Security," in Ashton B. Carter, John D. Steinbruner, and Charles A. Zraket, eds., *Managing Nuclear Operations* (Brookings, 1987), pp. 24–25; and Bruce G. Blair, "Alerting in Crisis and Conventional War," in ibid., p. 88, n. 28.
5. William W. Kaufmann, *Glasnost, Perestroika, and U.S. Defense Spending* (Brookings, 1990), table 10.

CHAPTER THREE

THE NEW ENVIRONMENT

THE DEFENSE BUDGET for fiscal 1990 went to Congress early in 1989. Within a matter of months, Soviet control over Eastern Europe began to unravel. A little more than two years later, it has become evident that the cold war has either ended or been replaced by a long truce. As a consequence, most of the data and assumptions that have done so much to shape U.S. force planning have come into question.

Nuclear Threats

Admittedly, Soviet strategic nuclear forces retain their imposing capabilities, and concerns exist about their control under a more decentralized Soviet regime. But modernization of these forces has slowed, and steps appear to be under way to reduce the ballistic missile and bomber components sufficiently to accommodate the constraints of the newly signed strategic arms treaty. Hence, although the formal threat remains, indications are growing that Gorbachev and his colleagues not only have lost interest in destroying the United States but would also welcome the end of a competition that has brought neither side any meaningful advantage and has reached this dead end at considerable and perhaps unnecessary cost to both.

As early as 1986, it had also become evident that Gorbachev and other Soviet leaders had lost their taste for the competition over other nuclear forces. With the ratification of the treaty on intermediate-range nuclear forces, they accepted the destruction of the land-based ballistic missiles that fell into this category, even though they surrendered a marked numerical advantage in doing so. In virtually the same breath, they indicated that they would welcome the elimination of all shorter-

Table 3-1. Non-Soviet Warsaw Pact Forces, 1990

Country	Military personnel	Divisions	Combat aircraft
Bulgaria	157,800	6	255
Czechoslovakia	197,000	10	450
German Democratic Republic	172,000	6	330
Hungary	99,000	5	135
Poland	406,000	13	625
Romania	179,500	10	350
Total	1,211,300	50	2,145

Source: Adapted from International Institute for Strategic Studies, *The Military Balance, 1988–1989* (Autumn 1988), pp. 46–53.

range nuclear capabilities. For the first time since the beginning of the cold war, the nuclear threat was actually decreasing rather than increasing.

Non-nuclear Threats

However striking these developments were, they hardly compared with what was happening to the non-nuclear threat. In this realm, at least three remarkable changes took place. First, the six Eastern European members of the Warsaw Pact broke free of Soviet control; they dissolved the Warsaw Pact; and a force of 1.2 million people, fifty divisions, and more than 2,100 combat aircraft could no longer be considered, even by NATO, as an integral part of the enemy's order of battle (table 3-1). Second, the USSR began to withdraw its forces from eastern Germany and completed their withdrawal from Hungary and Czechoslovakia. The departure from Germany is to be completed in 1994, by which time the two Soviet divisions remaining in Poland also will presumably have returned to the USSR. Third, the treaty on Conventional Forces in Europe (CFE)—covering almost all land-based non-nuclear capabilities from the Atlantic to the Urals—is now an accomplished fact. It will require the Soviet Union to destroy approximately 11,700 tanks, 12,000 armored vehicles, 19,300 artillery pieces, perhaps as many as 750 helicopters, and nearly 400 combat aircraft.[1]

Exactly how the Soviets will reconfigure their non-nuclear forces to accommodate these reductions remains to be seen. However, the number of Soviet divisions west of the Urals might well fall from 135

Table 3-2. Soviet Ground Forces, before and after Treaty on Conventional Forces in Europe

Military districts	Divisions in 1990		Estimated post-CFE divisions and tanks		
	Tank	Motorized rifle	Tank	Motorized rifle	Tanks
Leningrad	. . .	11	. . .	5½	678
Baltic	3	7	1	<5	839
Byelorussia	9	3	4	1	1,182
Carpathia	3	9	1	6	988
Kiev	9	7	4	4	1,513
Odessa	. . .	8	. . .	7	926
Moscow	1	7	1	2½	559
Volga/Urals	1	7	1	2½	559
North Caucasus	1	6	1	5	861
Trans-Caucasus	. . .	12	. . .	11	1,389
Groups of forces	16	14	10	13	4,500
Total	43	91	23	62½	13,994

Source: International Institute for Strategic Studies, *The Military Balance, 1990–1991*, p. 231.

to 86, a reduction of 36 percent. Of that total, according to one estimate, only 5 instead of 11 divisions would remain oriented toward Norway, while the threat to the critical central region of NATO would decline from as many as 111 (including 31 Eastern European divisions) to no more than 48 less powerful Soviet divisions drawn from the groups of forces and the Baltic, Byelorussian, Carpathian, Moscow, and Volga/Urals military districts (table 3-2).

Because the CFE treaty was negotiated while the Warsaw Pact still formally existed, and Eastern European forces were still counted as part of its total, the threat to NATO is now sixty-three divisions smaller than U.S. planners had originally assumed. Consequently, a short-warning attack on NATO has turned into an obsolete scenario, and it has become equally difficult to imagine the post-CFE Soviet forces successfully marching through Eastern Europe and defeating the remaining NATO ground and tactical air capabilities. It is little wonder, in these circumstances, that even the Pentagon has conceded that it would take the Soviet marshals two years or more to prepare for such a campaign.[2]

Such an estimate may actually prove too conservative. The Soviet armed forces are already in some disrepair, and their troubles appear to be mounting. Debates have erupted about the future role and missions of the Red Army. Efforts to conscript the usual number of young men have met with increasing resistance from some of the Soviet republics. And, as best can be calculated, the Soviet defense budget has gone into a fairly steep real decline. None of this is a foundation for highly ready forces, poised to take the offensive.

The gradual reversal of the Soviet role in a number of regional disputes and conflicts is almost as significant for the purposes of force planning as these other developments. After a decade of frustration, Soviet forces have withdrawn from Afghanistan. Moscow, as well as Washington, continues to provide aid to its clients in the conflict. But the civil war is no longer a major bone of contention. In fact, the USSR in cooperation with the United States has sought with some success to settle conflicts in Namibia, Angola, Ethiopia, and Cambodia. Equally satisfactory from the standpoint of the United States, Moscow has stopped or reduced its assistance to a number of its clients—including Nicaragua and Cuba—and proved an essential member of the coalition against Iraq.

Then there is the situation in the Soviet Union itself. A deteriorating economy, dissension over the course of the Kremlin's foreign and domestic policies, ethnic disputes, an abortive coup, and resistance by the Soviet republics to the central directives of Moscow have brought about a remarkable series of political changes and may even lead to major economic reforms. The exact role the Kremlin will play in foreign and defense policy continues to evolve. However, it is clear that the armed forces will continue to shrink and that the republics, as well as Gorbachev, will adhere to the START and CFE treaties. No one can doubt that a revolutionary and irresistible process is under way.

By 1990 even Secretary of Defense Cheney acknowledged a major reduction in the Soviet threat. In accordance with that bow to reality, he agreed that a smaller U.S. presence in Europe would be acceptable, and he directed force planners to remove the Soviet Union as the designated threat to the stability of the Middle East. How much effect the changes would have on the defense budget remained to be decided.

Endnotes

1. Alan Riding, "Baker Hopes Agreement Leads to Progress on Nuclear-Arms Cuts," *New York Times*, June 2, 1991, pp. A1, A12.
2. *Department of Defense Annual Report, Fiscal Year 1992*, p. 3.

CHAPTER FOUR

THE INITIAL DEBATE

NOT ALL OF THESE developments had come to pass in the early months of 1990 when Congress began its debate over the president's budget for fiscal 1991 (scheduled to take effect on October 1, 1990). As had been the case for the five previous years, the president faced a growing federal deficit, continued congressional pressure for lower defense spending and increases in domestic programs, and uncertainty within the executive branch about the future course of Soviet policy. In an effort at compromise, President George Bush proposed that authority for national defense decline in real terms by slightly more than 11 percent during the coming five years (1991 to 1995). The Congressional Budget Office (CBO), however, estimated that the defense program would cost $100 billion more (in constant dollars) than the president had recommended. This would mean approximately zero real growth rather than a projected reduction.

The problem, as defined by the CBO, was twofold. Prior-year balances of budget authority were continuing to convert into future expenditures at a high rate, owing to the heavy emphasis on procurement during the 1980s. This alone meant that, without other adjustments, the armed forces would become more modern and more expensive to maintain and operate. In addition, a gap existed, despite Secretary Cheney's efforts to reduce it, between the Pentagon's five-year defense program (FYDP) and the budgets that were being proposed. Adding to the problem, several independent analysts were suggesting that it should prove possible to cut defense spending in half by the year 2000 without any risk to national security.

Against this background, the House and Senate Budget committees began to consider different national defense budgets and major cuts of their own. In fact, the House Budget Committee proposed a FYDP

22   Decisions for Defense

Table 4-1. National Defense Budgets (050) Proposed in 1990 for Fiscal Years 1990-95
Billions of 1992 dollars

Source of proposal	1990	1991	1992	1993	1994	1995	1991-95
Congressional Budget Office							
Budget authority	327.7	322.8	326.0	325.6	325.5	326.2	1,626.1
Outlays	324.7	316.0	315.9	313.2	316.2	325.3	1,586.6
Defense Department (1/91)							
Budget authority	. . .	315.7	312.5	305.4	298.0	292.8	1,524.4
Outlays	. . .	313.1	309.2	300.2	295.3	285.4	1,503.2
Defense Department (revised 4/90)							
Budget authority	. . .	313.2	. . .	. . .	. . .	. . .	. . .
Outlays	. . .	313.0	. . .	. . .	. . .	. . .	. . .
House budget resolution							
Budget authority	. . .	291.1	280.5	264.9	250.6	237.4	1,324.5
Outlays	. . .	304.7	287.5	267.0	254.6	237.9	1,351.7
Senate Budget Committee							
Budget authority	. . .	293.8	285.4	274.5	264.6	255.2	1,373.5
Outlays	. . .	303.0	289.9	274.1	265.6	252.4	1,385.0
Senator Sam Nunn							
Budget authority	. . .	296.5	290.9	280.0	. . .	. . .	1,400.1
Outlays	. . .	306.2	295.0	280.7	. . .	. . .	1,408.1

Source: House Budget Committee, June 1990. Department of Defense deflators were used to convert current dollars into 1992 dollars.

that would have cut budget authority for national defense (in constant dollars) by 27.6 percent and spending by almost as much. The Senate Budget Committee was considering a similar FYDP in late spring of 1990 when the administration agreed to negotiate almost all the major elements of the federal budget. The hope was to reduce the federal deficit and resolve the long-standing dispute over the relative merits of domestic and defense spending (table 4-1).

A number of events shaped the outcome of the long and arduous discussions that followed. Secretary Cheney offered a 25 percent reduction in U.S. forces during the five-year planning period but argued that he could cut only 10 percent from budget authority. Senator Sam Nunn of Georgia, the influential chairman of the Senate Armed Services Committee, volunteered larger budgetary reductions of his own, although they were not as deep as those recommended by the House Budget Committee. Warnings began to sound that a recession was in the offing. And on August 2, 1990, Iraq seized Kuwait. The buildup of U.S. forces in Saudi Arabia began on August 4.

Table 4-2. National Defense (050) Targets for Fiscal Years 1990–96 Set in Budget Enforcement Act of 1990 and Administration Proposal of January 1991
Billions of 1992 dollars

| | Budget Enforcement Act | | Administration proposal | |
Year	Budget authority	Outlays	Budget authority	Outlays
1990	327.7	324.7	327.7	324.7
1991	296.6	306.2	293.8	308.2
1992	290.9	295.0	290.8	295.2
1993	280.0	280.8	279.8	280.7
1994	. . .	. . .	270.5	265.3
1995	. . .	. . .	263.8	257.5
1996	. . .	. . .	256.8	252.5

Sources: Table 5-5; and *Budget of the United States Government, Fiscal Year 1992*, pp. 4-4, 5-5.

Several major decisions about the defense budget and the FYDP soon followed this sequence of events. First, the congressional conferees and the executive branch mandated a major reduction in national defense for fiscal 1991. In real terms, budget authority would fall 9.5 percent from the funding appropriated for 1990. Outlays, however, would decline by only 5.7 percent, in part because of the large balances of prior-year budget authority still on the books. The incremental costs of the deployment to Saudi Arabia (and subsequently of Desert Storm) would be dealt with separately from the regular defense budget. The second decision resolved the disputes over the size of the federal budget and, to some degree, over its allocation by means of a comprehensive four-year plan, the Budget Enforcement Act of 1990, passed in October 1990 (table 4-2).

This rather complex legislation essentially exempted such entitlement programs as social security and medicare from any controls. However, it established overall ceilings on the federal budget for the four years after fiscal 1991 and, for 1992 and 1993, placed caps on the funding of three major budgetary categories: discretionary domestic programs, international affairs, and national defense.[1] The legislation also specified that even if appropriations for one of these categories fell below the ceiling for 1992 and 1993, a transfer of funds to another category would be forbidden. In other words, the law provided no incentive in the first two years to go below the caps and thereby reduce the federal deficit still further. In fiscal 1994 and 1995, however, the restrictions would change. Overall ceilings on the federal budget would remain, but the caps on the three discretionary categories would be lifted. Thus Congress could make trades among the programs for discretionary domestic needs, international affairs, and national defense. Presumably the pool of resources available for the three categories would be fixed each year; only the shares allocated to each could be varied.

The ceilings set for national defense in fiscal 1992 and 1993 imply real declines, respectively, of 1.9 percent and 3.8 percent in budget authority and 3.7 percent and 4.8 percent in outlays (table 4-2). The law did not specify how the Pentagon was to make these cuts. But members of Congress impressed on Secretary Cheney the need for a new national strategy that responded to the changed international environment in general and the vanishing Soviet threat in particular. They also asked for a FYDP that truly reflected the funds likely to be made available for defense.

Endnote

1. The budget for national defense includes funds for the Defense Department, the military applications of atomic energy (carried in the budget of the Energy Department), the strategic stockpile, and the selective service system.

CHAPTER FIVE

THE PENTAGON PLAN

IN JANUARY 1991 the Pentagon responded to congressional desires for
more realistic plans, programs, and budgets by providing a six-year
FYDP (now called future-years defense program), which formally
presents only the funds requested for the first five years (1992–96).
Officials also discussed the strategic concept and in March 1991
published an assessment of how the reduced non-nuclear forces
proposed by Secretary Cheney would perform in the new international
environment. Exactly how they arrived at the strategic concept and
derived the proposed force structure remains a matter of some
speculation. What is clear, however, is that most of the planning phase
was completed before the bombing of Iraq began.

The World According to Cheney

To say that the result sounds somewhat dated is not to criticize
the planners so much as the planning process. So complicated,
bureaucratized, unwieldy, and snail-paced has the process become that
its output is usually obsolete by the time the Pentagon presents it to
Congress. Secretary Cheney offered one example of this obsolescence
as late as March 1991. In his characterization of the new international
environment, he noted that "the Warsaw Pact is dead as a military
organization and the threat of a short-warning, global war starting in
Europe is now less likely than at any time in the last forty five years."
He also acknowledged that "the Soviet ability to project conventional
power beyond its borders will continue to decline."[1]
That was as up to date as he got. The archaic views were more
plentiful. According to the secretary, "the Soviet military will remain,

by a wide margin, the largest armed force on the [European] continent."
Even worse, "the Soviets not only retain significant strategic capability
but they are modernizing it virtually across the board."[2] Presumably
the large cuts that the Soviets have agreed to make in their non-nuclear
forces are of no account; nor are the programs to modernize all three
legs of the U.S. strategic triad.

The USSR was not the only source of the secretary's concerns. In
a quick update, he noted that the "Gulf conflict [Desert Storm] has
illustrated once again that . . . regional crises and conflicts are likely
to . . . escalate unpredictably, on very short notice, and often far from
home." Moreover, they would probably involve unidentified "foes well-
armed with elements of advanced conventional and unconventional
weaponry" and take place in "areas of interest to the United States."
There were, he said somewhat less vaguely, perennial challenges all
the way from Korea to the Persian Gulf, in other crisis locations in
the Middle East, and elsewhere.[3]

More specifically, the joint military net assessment (prepared by the
Joint Staff of the Chairman of the Joint Chiefs of Staff) described five
possible contingencies that could require the intervention of U.S.
non-nuclear forces: a "light" insurgency or narcotics activity in an
unspecified location; a lesser regional contingency, also "light," and
unidentified by country or region; a major regional contingency with
a "heavy" threat from North Korea; another major contingency in the
Middle East with a "heavy" threat from a revived and even more
aggressive Iraq; and worst of all, a war escalating from a European
crisis and involving a "heavy" threat, presumably from the USSR.
These contingencies might arise anywhere from 2,000 to 8,000 nautical
miles from the continental United States. Warning of them—apparently
to U.S. forces that they should prepare for intervention—would be
only a matter of days, thus requiring highly ready active-duty forces
and increased airlift.[4]

The Strategic Concept

Based on this projection of the international environment, Secretary
Cheney laid out what was to be the new U.S. strategic concept.
First, the strategic nuclear forces should be able to achieve effective

deterrence by persuading a potential aggressor that the cost of an attack on the United States or its allies would exceed by far any expected gain. Second, the strategic forces should be designed so as to strengthen nuclear stability, that is, so that no nation would feel under pressure to use nuclear weapons preemptively. Third, if deterrence should fail, U.S. capabilities should be survivable in sufficient numbers to permit a flexible and effective reply to the aggressor. Apparently this last injunction meant being able to respond to any level of aggression and to maintain options with respect to the timing and scale of a nuclear engagement, in the hope of reestablishing deterrence at the lowest possible level of violence. Assuring such a capability, which would include at least some ballistic missile defenses, would prove especially important with the proliferation of ballistic missiles with intercontinental range.[5]

The non-nuclear forces of the United States (presumably in conjunction with allies) should also seek to deter and respond to possible attacks, according to Cheney. How many contingencies might occur simultaneously, and in how many separate theaters the United States should prepare to become engaged at any one time, was not made clear. However, the assumption appears to be that the Pentagon should have the capability to deal with at least two major regional contingencies of the kind outlined by the joint military net assessment. At the same time, forces should be available to meet other defense needs, such as a forward presence, that is, land-based and sea-based forces deployed overseas in sensitive areas such as Europe and the Republic of Korea.[6]

To reinforce the "requirement" for these forces, Cheney asserted that the United States "cannot, under any circumstances, go below the minimum level necessary to protect U.S. interests and continue to play a leading role in shaping international events." He warned that the lower force levels he had proposed in the negotiation with Congress in 1990 were based on the assumption that the positive trends in the Soviet Union and the third world would continue. However, he noted that recent events in both areas had raised concerns—so much so that if developments in either region should take a turn for the worse, it might become necessary to slow the budgetary decline or possibly keep spending at more robust levels than he was then projecting. Even so, he acknowledged that if "the Soviets were to shift direction again and return to a strategy of military confrontation it would take them at least one or two years or longer to regenerate the capability for a European theater-wide offensive or a global conflict."[7]

Not inappropriately, the assistant secretary of defense for public affairs also asserted that the defense budgets for fiscal 1992 and 1993 reflected priorities that flowed directly from the new strategic concept. These priorities included nuclear deterrence through strong offensive forces, together with strategic and tactical defense systems; the forces and the transportation to project military power rapidly to areas of U.S. strategic interest; the ability to reconstitute a larger military posture, if needed; traditional high readiness at least for the active-duty forces; a vigorous research and development program; the timely deployment of advanced military systems; and the preservation of the industrial and technological base for continued military strength.[8]

Force Structure

Despite these assertions, it is probable, and indeed more comprehensible, that the reduced force structure emerged before the strategic concept. Active-duty military personnel are to decrease from 2,070,000 in 1990 to 1,653,000 in 1995. The selected reserve component (the National Guard and Reserves) will shrink from 1,128,000 to 906,000. And the civilian work force is to fall from 1,068,000 to 940,000 direct hires (table 5-1). Although not all the data on future force size and composition have been released, it is possible to see the general dimensions of the changes to be made in the capabilities that existed in 1990.

Strategic Nuclear Forces

The strategic nuclear forces will begin a modest contraction in anticipation of a strategic arms reduction treaty (START). The single-warhead Minuteman II ICBMs will be gradually phased out, as will the B-52G heavy bombers and nearly half the remaining Poseidon submarines and missiles (table 5-2). A triad of 550 ICBMs, 181 bombers, and 520 Poseidon (C-4) and Trident SLBMs will constitute the offensive force by 1995, for a total of 1,251 launchers with 9,780 warheads, of which slightly more than 8,000 will remain accountable under the terms

Table 5-1. Planned Reductions in Defense Military and Civilian Personnel, Selected Fiscal Years, 1987–95ª
Thousands of persons

	Type of personnel						
	Active military						
Year	*Army*	*Navy*	*Marine Corps*	*Air Force*	*Total*	*Selected reserves*	*Civilians*ᵇ
1987	781	587	199	607	2,174	1,151	1,133
1990	751	583	197	539	2,070	1,128	1,068
1992	660	551	188	487	1,886	1,068	1,003
1993	618	536	182	458	1,795	989	976
1994	577	516	176	445	1,714	924	958
1995	536	510	171	437	1,653	906	940
1987–95	−245	−77	−28	−170	−521	−245	−193
Percent reduction	31	13	14	28	24	21	17

Sources: Office of the Assistant Secretary of Defense (Public Affairs), "FY 1992–93 Department of Defense Budget Request," News Release 52-91 (February 4, 1991); and *Department of Defense Annual Report, Fiscal Year 1992*, p. 113.
a. At end of year.
b. Includes direct and indirect hires. *Department of Defense Annual Report* reports direct hires only.

of the START agreement. Since the Trident component of the triad will increase to 18 submarines and 432 launchers after 1995, either the ICBM force will have to decrease still further to meet the START limit of 4,900 warheads on ballistic missiles, or the removal of some warheads from selected missile launchers (called "downloading") will have to be allowed.

If Congress approves, the strategic forces will undergo a substantial modernization during the coming ten years. The rail garrison (train-mobile) MX ICBM has been canceled, but funding has been provided for what is being called a "basing verification missile and train." The small ICBM (SICBM or Midgetman), intended to be movable on a large transporter, is now under development and could replace the Minuteman III toward the end of the decade.

The Pentagon also proposes to upgrade the heavy bomber force. Current plans call for acquiring 75 B-2A stealth bombers, an improved short-range attack missile (SRAM II), and as many as 1,440 advanced cruise missiles, which will have greater range and a smaller radar cross-section than the ALCM-B, the currently deployed air-launched

Table 5-2. Estimated Changes in Numbers and Costs of Major U.S. Forces, Fiscal Years 1990–95
Costs in billions of 1992 dollars

Item	1990 Number	1990 Cost	1995 Number	1995 Cost	Percentage change in cost
Strategic nuclear forces					
Minuteman II ICBMs	450	1.8	0	0	−100
Minuteman III ICBMs	500	2.7	500	2.7	0
MX ICBMs	50	2.0	50	2.0	0
Heavy bombers	268	13.2	181	9.5	−28
Poseidon launchers	368	6.1	160	2.7	−56
Trident C-4, D-5					
launchers	216	4.5	360	7.5	67
Non-nuclear forces					
Army divisions					
Active duty	18	70.3	12	46.9	−33
Reserve	10	9.3	6	5.6	−40
Marine brigades/wings					
Active duty	9/3	6.6	8/3	5.9	−11
Reserve	3/1	0.6	3/1	0.6	0
Air Force fighter wings					
Active duty	24	42.5	15	26.6	−37
Reserve	12	5.4	11	5.0	−7
Naval forces					
Carrier battle groups/					
ships	14/266	53.5	12/228	45.9	−14
Other battle force ships	279	29.5	223	23.6	−20
Total	. . .	248.0	. . .	184.5	−25.6

Sources: *Department of Defense Annual Report, Fiscal Year 1992*, pp. 115–17; Testimony of Robert D. Reischauer, director of Congressional Budget Office, before the House Committee on the Budget, February 27, 1991, table 5; and authors' estimates.

cruise missile. The defects of the B-1B bomber would be corrected as well.

More Trident submarines, the last of which was funded in fiscal 1991, will come into service, and the SLBM force will continue to receive a new, more powerful and accurate ballistic missile (the D-5) with the range of a modern ICBM. With the deployment of the D-5, in fact, the Trident leg of the triad will by itself have a high probability of destroying the full spectrum of fixed targets contained in the SIOP (single integrated operational plan), including the very hard targets that were once the sole province of ICBMs and bombers. The D-5 has the further advantages of survivability, long endurance, and sufficiently

Table 5-3. Major Modernization for Strategic Nuclear Forces, 1992–2001
Billions of current dollars

Program	Acquisition cost	Annual operating and support costs
B-2 stealth bomber	65.0	9.8
Small ICBM	13.5	1.4
D-5 SLBM	35.0	3.5
SSN-21 attack submarine	19.0	1.9
Strategic defense initiative (GPALS)	100.0	10.0
Total	232.5	26.6

Source: Authors' estimates.

good communications so that the national command authority (the president or one of his appointed successors) can withhold a portion or all of the missiles without fear of losing them.

Not content with these advances, which more than match what the Soviets are doing, the administration proposes continued development of an antisatellite system. More important, it plans to reorient the strategic defense initiative (also known as Star Wars and SDI) and increase the funding for it and for tactical ballistic missile defenses, which would upgrade the Patriot system. The reoriented SDI, now known by the amiable acronym of GPALS (global protection against limited strikes), will—like its more grandiose predecessor—consist of both space-based and surface-based sensors and interceptors. But, as its new name implies, it will be only half the size of its predecessor and cost perhaps only 80 percent as much. Indeed, if GPALS is deployed, along with all the other proposed strategic offensive and defensive systems, the acquisition costs alone will amount to $232 billion dollars over the next ten years (table 5-3). The operating and support costs for them could also be high.

Tactical Nuclear Forces

For contractors, the strategic forces may still look like a promising source of demand. By contrast, the market for what are now called the nonstrategic or substrategic nuclear capabilities appears to be catastrophically bad. The NATO heads of state, meeting in London in 1990, agreed that the warheads deployed for the shortest-range systems—mostly artillery—should be significantly reduced. Furthermore, once negotiations begin with the Soviet Union on short-range nuclear forces, NATO will propose to eliminate all nuclear ordnance from Europe in return for reciprocal action by the USSR.[9] That move, combined with the cancellation of the follow-on-to Lance (FOTL) missile, allegedly will force exclusive reliance on nuclear-capable aircraft and strengthen the case for the development of a tactical air-to-surface missile (TASM or SRAM-T) to provide these aircraft with the capability to attack heavily defended targets. Such targets will presumably be in the USSR, because it no longer seems appropriate to aim nuclear weapons at eastern Germany, Czechoslovakia, and Poland.

A peculiar view persists about the special virtues of land-based tactical nuclear weapons: that the president would be more willing to release them than their sea-based counterparts, and that the allies need to see and if necessary stroke these rather sinister guardians in order to have confidence in the American nuclear deterrent. However, there are substitutes for them. The Navy is already deploying a long-range standoff capability in the form of the nuclear Tomahawk land-attack missile (TLAM-N) on submarines and surface combatants that are far less vulnerable than airfields and aircraft. In short, land-based tactical nuclear systems and their warheads could soon be on their way to a well-deserved retirement.

Non-nuclear Forces

The non-nuclear forces appear to have a more promising future, especially after the military success of Desert Storm and the dominant role played in it by Air Force bombers and fighters. However, none of the services will escape the cut of the budgetary knife. The Army will go down from twenty-eight active and reserve divisions to eighteen. The Marine Corps will lose at least one of its active brigades and perhaps some of its aircraft. The Navy will shrink from 545 to 451 battle force ships, including 12 instead of 14 large aircraft carriers. The Air Force, despite its stunning performance in Iraq, will have to sacrifice ten of its thirty-six active and reserve fighter wings. In addition, Secretary Cheney has already terminated or proposes to

Table 5-4. Pentagon Allocation of U.S. Non-Nuclear Forces, 1995

Force	Atlantic command	Pacific command	Contingency command	Total
Army (divisions)				
Active duty	5	2	5	12
Reserve	6	. . .	. . .	6
Reconstitutable	2	. . .	. . .	2
Marine Corps (divisions/wings)				
Active	1/1	1/1	1/1	3/3
Reserve	1	. . .	. . .	1
Air Force (wings)				
Active	5	3	7	15
Reserve	11	. . .	. . .	11
Navy carriers	6	6	. . .	12

Sources: Michael R. Gordon, "Pentagon Drafts Strategy for Post-Cold War World," *New York Times*, August 2, 1990, pp. 1, 14; and Defense Budget Project, *Responding to Changing Threats: A Report of the Defense Budget Project's Task Force on the FY 1992–FY 1997 Defense Plan* (Washington, June 1991), p. 15.

cancel a number of familiar non-nuclear programs. They include the Army's M-1 tank, M-2 fighting vehicle, and AH-64 helicopter; the Navy's F-14 and A-12 aircraft; the Marine Corps' AV-8B jump jet and V-22 tilt-rotor aircraft; and even the Air Force's highly successful F-15E and F-16 fighters.

There will be some debate about whether, in the process of making all these cuts and cancellations, Cheney has closed the gap between the future-years defense program and the funds he has requested. As the CBO has pointed out, most of the cancellations are intended to make room for the next generation of weapons systems that are due for production in the later 1990s.[10]

Of equal interest is the way the reduced non-nuclear forces are allocated to the main planning contingencies (table 5-4). Although some doubt has arisen as to whether his proposal will survive interservice competition, General Colin L. Powell, chairman of the Joint Chiefs of Staff, has recommended that the theater command structure—Europe, Atlantic, Pacific, Southern, and Central—be reduced from five to three. The new command structure would consist of the Atlantic, Pacific and Contingency commands.

THE ATLANTIC COMMAND. The Atlantic command is to have the responsibility for armor-heavy attacks in Europe and southwest Asia (the current label for the Middle East and Persian Gulf). The forces allocated to it will apparently consist of five active-duty division equivalents, six National Guard divisions, and two cadre divisions (called "reconstitutable"), along with the equivalent of eighteen Air Force fighter wings (one Marine wing, because of its size, is counted as equal to two Air Force wings), six carrier battle groups, and other unspecified naval battle force ships and submarines. Of this total, two Army divisions and three to four Air Force fighter wings will remain in Europe, and one carrier battle group may be kept on station in the Mediterranean along with an afloat Marine battalion.

In an emergency, the Atlantic command would attempt, within ten days, to reinforce Europe with four Army divisions, ten Air Force fighter wings, and one Marine brigade, which would probably go to Norway. After two or three months, the remaining units could also reinforce Europe. As an alternative, five of these divisions with supporting fighter wings and naval forces could deploy to southwest Asia. In the event of simultaneous threats in Europe and the Persian Gulf, for example, at least five Army divisions and six Air Force fighter wings could be drawn from the Contingency command and committed to one of the two theaters within approximately six weeks. A European conflict is characterized as likely to be of medium to high intensity and to continue for more than 50 days. A war in southwest Asia is expected to be of the same intensity but last 120 days. The size and cost of the war reserve stocks of ammunition, other supplies, and equipment are not articulated. However, a European crisis would call for a full U.S. mobilization. The southwest Asia contingency by itself would require the callup of 200,000 reservists.[11]

THE PACIFIC COMMAND. The Pacific command appears to have the primary mission of contributing to the defense of South Korea and maintaining a military presence in the western Pacific. To execute these missions, the command is to be assigned the equivalent of three divisions, five Air Force fighter wing equivalents, six carrier battle groups, and other unspecified battle force ships. One slimmed-down Army division and perhaps a wing of Air Force fighters are to remain in Korea, while another division from Hawaii or Alaska would be available for reinforcement. So would four Marine brigades and their air support, located in Okinawa, Hawaii, and the United States. Perhaps as many as two to three Air Force fighter wings, located on bases in the Pacific, and one carrier battle group, home-ported in

Japan, could also serve as rapid reinforcements. Although the ground component of the force is likely to be relatively light in armor, the assumption is that, along with South Korean capabilities, it would face an armor-heavy North Korean attack in a war of medium to high intensity for as many as 120 days.[12]

THE CONTINGENCY COMMAND. The Contingency command sounds in many ways like the Central command revisited. Its main missions seem to arise from spontaneous and often unpredictable crises occurring in the third world. These crises could call for the use of special operations forces to counter terrorism, the export of narcotics, or insurgencies against friendly governments. Such crises could also lead to attacks of a more conventional character, some of which would require a rapid U.S. response with a relatively small but highly ready active-duty force of relative self-sufficiency

Other contingencies might be of more considerable size and sophistication and could occur in areas where the United States has no forward presence. Under these conditions, the contingency forces would act as the lead element in a major intervention, to be followed as necessary by heavier capabilities and the support for combat lasting as long as ninety days. No doubt the precedent of Desert Storm was much on the minds of the planners as they developed this last contingency. Indeed, it presumes a thoroughly revived and more aggressive Iraq whose leader manages this time to seize Kuwait and secure the oil fields and main points of access to Saudi Arabia. In the circumstances, it is hardly surprising to discover that six Army and Marine divisions are assigned to the Contingency command, and that three of them are the familiar 82nd Airborne, 101st Air Assault, and 24th Mechanized Infantry, which along with Marine units were the first to deploy to Saudi Arabia in 1990. The command would also contain seven Air Force fighter wings, a large Marine wing, a complement of B-52s configured to deliver non-nuclear ordnance, and an undisclosed number of special operations forces and the Navy's battle force ships.[13]

LOGISTICS. To support the rapid deployment of U.S. forces, 30,000 tons of Marine Corps matériel will continue to be stored in Norway. Another 400,000 tons or more of equipment and supplies will remain in central Europe to facilitate the rapid deployment of four U.S. divisions. In addition, the Marine Corps will have thirteen maritime pre-positioning ships, which, together with twelve Army and Air Force pre-positioning ships, will make available another 275,000 tons or more for use primarily in southwest Asia. Beyond that, the Ready Reserve Fleet will be increased from 96 cargo and tanker ships to 142, and will be kept in better readiness than it proved to be at the outset of Desert Shield. The Pentagon will also seek permission from various governments in the Persian Gulf to store pre-positioned matériel on land, establish access agreements, and develop coordinated planning, along with carrying out periodic U.S. deployments and joint exercises such as those conducted with Egypt. Finally, the Air Force will attempt to reach its goal of airlifting 60 million ton/miles a day. This will give total U.S. airlift—including the Civil Reserve Air Fleet— the capacity to deliver 13,000 tons a day to Europe and almost 8,000 a day to Saudi Arabia.[14]

These preparations, while impressive, may not be sufficient to support two major contingencies at the same time. One solution to the problem would be to acquire more sealift and less airlift, since in thirty days ten fast sealift ships could transport more cargo to Saudi Arabia than the entire airlift fleet. Another equally distasteful solution would be to tailor the forces to the size of the airlift and sealift and accept the reality of a one-war strategic concept.

Net Assessment

The Joint Staff's military net assessment not only recognizes the lift shortage, it also discusses the implications of this problem in its assessment of the risks associated with the projected threats and the proposed U.S. forces. Briefly, its conclusions are as follows: first, the forces will provide the minimum capability necessary to achieve U.S. national security objectives; second, owing to a number of problems, including the lift shortage, there is a moderately high but acceptable probability that these forces will not be able to perform their missions; and third, the armed forces, when reduced according to Secretary Cheney's plan, will be rapidly approaching an irreducible minimum. That is, if their capabilities were to be reduced further, the United States would either have to live with unacceptable risks or fundamentally alter its position in the world order and redefine its objectives and policies.

Table 5-5. Actual and Estimated Budgets for National Defense, by Appropriation Title, Fiscal Years 1990–96
Billions of 1992 dollars

Appropriation title	1990ᵃ	1991ᵇ	1992ᵇ	1993ᵇ	1994ᵇ	1995ᵇ	1996ᵇ
Military personnel	85.3	81.3	78.0	74.5	70.9	67.8	66.4
Operation and maintenance	95.4	88.5	86.5	81.5	78.4	76.6	75.9
Procurement	88.0	65.9	63.4	64.2	63.7	66.8	64.5
Research, development, test and evaluation	39.4	35.6	39.9	39.4	37.2	33.5	31.0
Military construction	5.5	5.1	4.5	3.6	6.5	5.7	5.7
Military family housing	3.3	3.4	3.6	3.5	3.7	3.5	3.4
Allowances	. . .	. . .	−0.3	−0.9	−4.4	−3.9	−3.7
Revolving and management funds	−0.3	1.0	2.7	1.5	1.8	1.0	0.5
Defense (051)	316.6	280.8	278.3	267.3	257.8	251.0	243.7
Atomic energy (053)	10.5	11.9	11.7	11.7	12.0	12.2	12.3
Other (054)	0.6	1.1	0.8	0.8	0.7	0.7	0.7
National defense (050)	327.7	293.8	290.8	279.8	270.5	263.9	256.7
National defense outlays (050)	324.7	308.2	295.2	280.7	265.3	257.5	252.5

Source: *Budget of the United States Government, Fiscal Year 1992*, pt. 2, pp. 190–91. Defense Department deflators were used to convert current dollars into 1992 dollars.
a. Actual.
b. Estimated.

In other words, the Joint Staff believes that it would be disastrous for the United States to make any further cuts in the proposed forces and their estimated costs.[15]

Costs

These rather dire warnings seem out of place. Despite the planned cuts in the forces and the many program cancellations and reductions, Secretary Cheney's recommended defense funding is not exactly marginal. In fact, the budget authority requested for defense between fiscal 1992 and 1996 (in 1992 dollars) will amount to nearly $1.3 trillion (table 5-5), with outlays expected to be only slightly lower. In addition, other activities directly related to defense—of which the Department of Energy's production of nuclear weapons and naval nuclear reactors is the largest—are estimated to need nearly $64 billion in budget authority and to result in outlays of $62 billion during the same five years. Yet it is claimed that unless the national defense function is allowed budget authority of $1,361.7 billion and expenditures of $1,351.2 billion (in 1992 dollars) in the five-year period, the United States will become a second-rate power in a new world order that is allegedly almost as dangerous as the old one.

The proposed allocation of these resources can best be shown by means of three different budget formats, all of which use budget authority as the most appropriate indicator of current and future policy. In order to display real trends, 1992 dollars are calculated for all the budgets, based on the Pentagon's estimates of inflation.

The first budget, broken down by appropriation title, is the only one of the three that has official sanction (table 5-5). From 1990 to 1996, national defense declines by just under 21.7 percent, while the Defense Department suffers a 23 percent reduction (somewhat more than Secretary Cheney originally proposed), largely because of the steep decline in 1991. The biggest loser is Pentagon procurement, which is cut by nearly 27 percent. The military personnel account takes the second biggest hit (a little more than 22 percent), and research, development, test, and evaluation (RDT&E) comes in third with a loss of 21.3 percent. Of the major accounts, operation and maintenance suffers the least, with a reduction of 20.4 percent.

More important, at least for the next few years, Cheney has cut the investment account (procurement, RDT&E, and military construction) by 24 percent and thereby produced a FYDP that bears a serious relationship to the resources he is likely to obtain. He has protected the funds for operation and support (military personnel, operation and maintenance, and military family housing), which go down less than 21 percent. Even though the trend may not last beyond 1996, he has reduced operation and maintenance less than military personnel, which suggests that he is giving combat readiness more than lip service.

It is more difficult to estimate how these cuts will affect the major categories of forces, in part because of a lack of data. However, under the Cheney plan, Army active-duty divisions will go from eighteen to twelve (a cut of 33 percent), and National Guard divisions will fall from a nominal ten to six (a cut of 40 percent) (table 5-2). By contrast, Air Force fighter wings shrink from approximately twenty-four to fifteen (for a reduction of more than 37 percent), while the Air National Guard would go down from twelve to eleven (a decline of little more

Table 5-6. Annual Cost of Force Planning Contingencies, Fiscal Years 1990 and 1996
Billions of 1992 dollars

Force planning contingency	1990	1996
Strategic nuclear deterrence	48.2	41.8
Tactical nuclear deterrence	2.4	1.5
Non-nuclear defense of:		
North Norway	16.7	12.2
Central Europe	90.3	44.0
Mediterranean	7.6	7.6
Atlantic sea lanes	21.7	21.7
Middle East/Persian Gulf	64.5	55.1
South Korea	19.0	17.3
Pacific sea lanes	14.7	14.7
Alaska	1.4	1.0
Panama and Caribbean	3.2	3.2
Continental United States	7.6	4.4
National intelligence and communications	19.2	19.2
Total (051)	316.5	243.7

Sources: Table 5-5; and authors' estimates.

than 8 percent). The Marine Corps gets off more lightly, with a cut of 13 percent in personnel, but what seems to be a reduction of only one brigade of its ground forces and no more than 11 percent of its air wings. The Navy, not including the Marine Corps, suffers a loss of slightly over 17 percent of its ships and 14 percent of its tactical aviation as the carriers go from fourteen to twelve. In all these calculations, it is assumed that the annual cost for airlift and sealift and national intelligence and communications will remain relatively constant, with the Air Force substituting a smaller number of C-17 aircraft for the older C141s, the Navy expanding its Ready Reserve Fleet, and a continuation of the gradual modernization of surveillance systems and satellite communications.

Because the forces will be distributed among four operational commands (including the strategic nuclear forces), it is not easy to compare them with the force distributions in 1990. However, if the notion is accepted that the Atlantic command essentially contains the forces intended for Europe and the Contingency command is simply the Central command with a new title, then a meaningful comparison of planning contingencies and costs becomes possible (table 5-6).

On this and other assumptions, the annual cost of U.S. nuclear forces (tactical as well as strategic) will fall from $50.6 billion in 1990 to $43.3 billion in 1996 (in 1992 dollars). The cost of north Norway drops from $16.7 billion to $12.2 billion. The defense of central Europe will also fall from $90.3 billion to $44.0 billion, the cost of the Mediterranean stays at $7.6 billion, and the price of the Atlantic remains a substantial $21.7 billion. In all, the U.S. contribution to the defense of Europe will still cost $85.5 billion a year in 1992 dollars, compared with $136.3 billion in 1990, and will represent 35 percent of the defense budget (or 33 percent of the budget for national defense). What is to become the Pacific command will have a budget of $33.0 billion (compared with $35.1 billion in 1990), with $17.3 billion for South Korea, $14.7 billion for the Pacific sea lanes, and $1.0 billion for Alaska. Assuming that the Contingency command will have the responsibility for all the remaining contingencies, with the Persian Gulf as the most prominent of them, its budget will come to $62.7 billion (against a comparable total of $75.3 billion in 1990), with $55.1 billion for the Persian Gulf, $3.2 billion for Panama and the Caribbean, and $4.4 billion for the CONUS. National intelligence and communications will retain its 1990 level of $19.2 billion.

Based on this set of assumptions, what is called the new strategy does not seem very different from the old. The costs of the key planning contingencies go down, but the Pentagon apparently sees the same potential crises in the same regions of the world. From this perspective, the new world is only slightly less threatening than the old one.

Endnotes

1. Department of Defense, *1991 Joint Military Net Assessment* (March 1991), pp. i, ii.

2. DOD, *1991 Joint Military Net Assessment*, p. ii.

3. DOD, *1991 Joint Military Net Assessment*, p. ii; and *Department of Defense Annual Report, Fiscal Year 1992*, p. 3.

4. DOD, *1991 Joint Military Net Assessment*, table 9-1, p. 9-2.

5. *Department of Defense Annual Report, Fiscal Year 1992*, pp. 51, 53–55, 59–60.

6. *Department of Defense Annual Report, Fiscal Year 1992*, p. 61.

7. *Department of Defense Annual Report, Fiscal Year 1992*, pp. 3–4.

8. Office of the Assistant Secretary of Defense (Public Affairs), "FY 1992–93 Department of Defense Budget Request," News Release 52-91 (February 4, 1991).

9. *Department of Defense Annual Report, Fiscal Year 1992*, p. 57.

10. Michael R. Gordon, "Pentagon Drafts Strategy for Post-Cold War World," *New York Times*, August 2, 1990, pp. 1, 14; *Department of Defense Annual Report, Fiscal*

Year 1992, p. 4; and Statement of Robert F. Hale, assistant director, National Security Division, Congressional Budget Office, before the House Committee on Armed Services, March 19, 1991, pp. 22–26.

11. DOD, *1991 Joint Military Net Assessment*, table 9-1, p. 9-2.

12. DOD, *1991 Joint Military Net Assessment*, table 9-1, p. 9-2.

13. DOD, *1991 Joint Military Net Assessment*, pp. 2–10; and Gordon, "Pentagon Drafts Strategy."

14. *Department of Defense Annual Report, Fiscal Year 1992*, pp. 77–81.

15. DOD, *1991 Joint Military Net Assessment*, p. 9-9.

CHAPTER SIX

ISSUES

WILLIAM R. INGE, the "gloomy" dean of Saint Paul's Cathedral in London, once wrote, "When our first parents were driven out of Paradise, Adam is believed to have remarked to Eve: 'My dear, we live in an age of transition.'"[1] Much the same comment could be made about the international environment and the Pentagon's plans for the 1990s. The United States has been cast out of the familiar surroundings of the cold war and has begun to search for a new world order as the basis for an appropriate defense strategy and force structure. The FYDP presented by Secretary Cheney early in 1991 represents one approach to this difficult task. Unfortunately, it raises more issues than it purports to resolve. High on the list of these issues are the realism of the environment postulated by the secretary, the effect of changing the assumptions about the environment on the recommended plans and programs, and the realism of the FYDP, particularly if newer weapons come into the defense inventory.

The Nature of the Trends

Essentially, the view from the Pentagon is of a scaled-down version of the cold war. The Soviets still are believed to constitute enough of a threat to warrant a U.S. strategic nuclear force that has only 19 percent fewer warheads in 1995 than it did in 1990 and costs only 13 percent less (in 1992 dollars). The USSR also provides the rationale for 14 Army and Marine Corps divisions (of which 2 would be reconstitutable), 6 carrier battle groups, half or more of some 220 other battle force ships (mostly surface combatants and nuclear attack submarines), and on the order of 16 Air Force fighter wings. Yet it seems highly likely that the number of nuclear targets in the Soviet Union that could be covered or are worth covering with U.S. second-strike forces is shrinking as the Soviets continue to move from silo-based to mobile ICBMs, as their fragile economy becomes more easily disrupted by the destruction of a small number of targets, and as a larger percentage of U.S. warheads is concentrated in the highly survivable Trident submarines, meaning more deliverable (and with-holdable) warheads. Indeed, the current strategic arms reduction treaty, which has taken so many years to negotiate, can and should be followed quickly with further START negotiations accompanied by less formal agreements to engage in mutual reductions. Such a step is in the interest of both countries and would run a very low risk once the START and CFE verification regimes go into effect.

Even more dramatic developments are affecting the U.S. non-nuclear forces. Soviet ground and tactical air units are withdrawing from central and Eastern Europe and probably will have completed their return to the USSR by the end of 1994. The Soviet Union's armed forces are already in turmoil as a consequence of unilateral cuts instituted by Gorbachev, resistance to conscription, internal disputes, and the reduced production of military hardware, the most modern of which the Ministry of Defense appears eager to sell to anyone with the necessary hard currency. The further cuts in Soviet forces required by the CFE treaty, combined with the dissolution of the Warsaw Pact, make it difficult to understand why so many divisions and air wings have to be allocated to the defense of a Western Europe that may not wish to live alone in the long shadow of a united Germany and a chaotic USSR, but is fully capable of providing for its own defense.

It may make sense on several grounds for the United States to maintain a small non-nuclear presence in Western Europe if the allies so desire and to keep a modest complement of ground and tactical air forces to reinforce it. But it has become increasingly difficult to visualize what might happen in Europe in the foreseeable future that would justify a U.S. commitment nearly as large as that deemed necessary during the cold war. So far, at least, neither the secretary of defense nor the Joint Staff has provided a persuasive explanation.

How Many Iraqs?

The prospects for peace and stability in Europe apparently look poor to the Pentagon, but the future in southwest Asia looks even worse. Planners clutch the image of a powerful and belligerent Saddam Hussein despite the devastation wrought on Iraq and its armed forces in early 1991. As a consequence, not only do they give the Atlantic command the alternative mission of intervening in southwest Asia with heavy active-duty forces; they also provide the Contingency command with six divisions and the equivalent of nine fighter wings and, depending on the circumstances, the right to draw on the Atlantic and Pacific commands for naval and other forces. In effect, this allows for a replay of Desert Storm yet provides a comfortable cushion for other less probable contingencies.

The difficulties with this scenario and its implications for the U.S. force structure are manifold. Given the defeat of Iraq and the effects of the embargo imposed on it, it seems at best improbable that Baghdad would recover sufficiently to resume its aggressive behavior during the next ten years. In any event, there is a high probability that the United States overinsured in its deployment of ground and tactical air forces to the Persian Gulf area in 1990 simply because the entire inventory of U.S. non-nuclear capabilities was available for use. Certainly it is hard to argue that six carrier battle groups were essential to the success of the campaign. Furthermore, if Iraq is scratched from the list of serious future threats, it is not easy to find a substitute with the same capabilities and intentions, or such weak allies, in an area vital to the United States. There are, of course, candidates such as Iran or Syria, and some might even say Israel. But the likelihood seems rather low for the next ten years that any one of them could or would want to replace Iraq—especially after the awesome, if excessive, display of U.S. military power. Only Iran has the wallet for such an enterprise. But there is little evidence that it has the will, knowing how closely scrutinized its behavior has become and what U.S. reaction might lie in store for it.

To justify a non-nuclear force of the size that Secretary Cheney is projecting, the Pentagon must do better than simply assume a replay of Desert Storm. At a minimum, planners should produce more realistic threats than they have done so far. They might also wish to demonstrate that Desert Storm could not have produced the same outcome with fewer ground, air, and naval forces. Furthermore, it would help if they could show that the Atlantic and Pacific commanders would be so preoccupied with other dangers at the same time that they could not, if necessary, provide all the capabilities necessary to replicate Desert Storm.

Obviously, despite a historical record of forty-five years, one cannot say that the probability of simultaneous confrontations in areas critical to the security and well-being of the United States is zero. But, as General Colin Powell has remarked, "I would be very surprised if another Iraq occurred." He went on to say, "Think hard about it, I'm running out of demons. I'm running out of villains. . . . I'm down to Castro and Kim Il Sung."[2] Such a list does not hold out much hope for several more or less simultaneous contingencies of any consequence. Nor does it suggest that the United States should pay a high premium to insure against eventualities of such low probability, given what President Bush has described as a shortage of wallet.

North Korea and Cuba

This is not to deny that North Korea and Cuba can create problems for the allies and other friends of the United States. In the manner touted by the Soviet Union of old, the North Koreans painfully support armed forces of considerable size, estimated by U.S. intelligence at 1.1 million people, 3,000 tanks, and 800 combat aircraft. On the face of it, as in the case of Iraq, the numbers are frightening. But the situation on the Korean peninsula differs from that in Saudi Arabia in 1990. A supposedly smaller but highly trained South Korean force with modern equipment and large reserves lies behind one of the most heavily fortified lines in the world. Moreover, it seems increasingly unlikely that the North Koreans could count on Chinese or Soviet support for an invasion of the south.

For twenty years, a strong minority in and out of the Pentagon has argued that Seoul, with its larger population and expanding economy, could by itself prove more than a military match for Pyongyang. At the risk of being tactless, it might even be argued that the main reason for a U.S. military presence in South Korea is to keep a rein on the leadership in Seoul and prevent it from developing nuclear weapons or preparing an invasion of the north.

Be that as it may, Pentagon planners still assume that South Korea will need considerable support from the United States in order to repel a full-scale invasion from the north. It is as though North Korea, like an attack dog, would surely leap at the southern jugular were it not for the restraining leash of deterrence provided by the South Korean forces, a U.S. presence, and the prospect that land, air, and naval reinforcements would rapidly deploy to the theater. According to General Powell, "There are not any real major threats out there, with the possible exception of Korea." And yet as far as he is concerned, "We're not going to get in a major war on the Asian land mass any time soon."[3]

At a minimum, therefore, the issue is whether the Pentagon should continue to subsidize the defense of South Korea. If the answer is that it must do so to forestall nuclear proliferation, hold the South Korean government in check, and contribute to the security of Japan, the issue then becomes not whether but how large a subsidy is required for these purposes. Does the United States really need to keep on spending more than $17 billion a year (in 1992 dollars) to police the area, or could it achieve the same results with fewer forces and lower cost? The warmer relations of the USSR and China with South Korea, combined with economic difficulties in the north and a slightly greater display of flexibility in foreign policy by Pyongyang, make it essential that time-worn defense planning assumptions about the Pacific undergo a much more serious review than has taken place thus far.

Since the electoral defeat of the Sandanistas in Nicaragua and the U.S. intervention in Panama, the Bush administration has shown a relaxed attitude toward events in the Caribbean and Central America. But it would appear from General Powell's remarks that the Pentagon still sees a possible need to draw on forces from the Contingency command to deal with any trouble Castro might cause in his general vicinity. Perhaps that is still a necessary precaution. But one wonders whether anything beyond special operations forces would be needed, and how much taste Castro will have for foreign adventures when his patron in the Kremlin is reducing his subsidy and demanding hard currency as well as sugar in return for its remaining support. Indeed, with domestic problems increasing, Castro appears to have become more of a threat to his own people than to other countries in the region.

An Irreducible Minimum?

Because of the somewhat artificial and exaggerated portrayal of the threats underlying the Pentagon's strategic concept and the proposed U.S. force structure, the authors of the joint military net assessment have nothing but grim news about the future. From their perspective, the forces planned for the latter part of the 1990s, especially the non-nuclear forces, can handle the future threats with a high but acceptable risk, whatever that means. But they also describe the programmed forces as an irreducible minimum. To cut further, they say—having abandoned all estimates of risk or probability—will force the United States to reduce its commitments and retreat to less acceptable goals for its foreign and defense policies.[4] General Powell, in a less apocalyptic version of the same reasoning, suggests that going below the irreducible minimum will tear off the epaulets of the United States as a superpower and oblige it to forfeit its role of world leader. According to Powell, "You've got to step aside from the context we've been using for the past forty years, that you base [military planning] against a specific threat. We no longer have the luxury of having a threat to plan for. What we plan for is that we're a superpower. We are the major player on the world stage with responsibilities [and] interests around the world."[5]

That there is such a thing as an irreducible minimum for the armed forces of the United States, or that a force structure can be systematically inferred from stamping the United States as a superpower, would be a difficult proposition to demonstrate, much less prove. An equally plausible argument might maintain that the Joint Staff has no business dictating what is an acceptable risk, and that real superpowers not only refuse to eat quiche but also decline to pass the hat to pay for their wars. The president might well decide that the risk was acceptable, although high, because the probability of conflict was so low. He might also note that the Joint Staff's statement of risk, however contrived, depends on gloomy assumptions about the dangers of the future and a conservative view of the forces needed to meet them. If the president were to assume, not unreasonably, that during the next ten years no more than one serious threat at a time would confront the United States, the irreducible minimum of forces would fall well below the floor set by the Joint Staff, and yet the assessment of risk might actually decline.

In sum, as General Powell has intimated, the new world order could well differ radically from the cold war era in its demands for U.S. military capabilities. Conflicts there will undoubtedly be, just as domestic violence remains a scourge. But in the next ten years, few such disturbances are likely to jeopardize the core conditions of U.S. security or, after Desert Storm, the military reputation of the United States, unless the Pentagon uses its resources in a grossly inefficient way. The true test of the United States as a superpower will be whether it can now arrive at a more realistic balance between its military and economic power than it has done in the recent past.

Future Resource Constraints

Even if one accepts the force structure proposed by the Pentagon as the irreducible minimum, a major issue remains. It is by no means clear that Secretary Cheney's program to modernize and transport the scaled-down forces will fit within the resource constraints he has accepted, much less the budget authority the Pentagon is likely to receive from Congress after fiscal 1991. For the short run, the secretary has acted more courageously than most of his predecessors in stretching out and terminating a long list of programs, most of them designed to modernize the forces with the current generation of weapons. In doing so, he has relaxed the upward pressure on defense budgets that has come from rushing weapons into production before they were fully tested and from piggy-backing systems one on top of another so that all of them arrived simultaneously at the most expensive stage of the investment process—series production. It is true that the large balances of prior-year budget authority, consisting mostly of funds committed to procurement but not yet spent, will continue to disgorge new weapons for some years to come and increase operating and support costs (table 6-1). But over the next five years the stretchouts, cancellations, and force reductions mandated by Secretary Cheney will probably compensate for most, if not all, of these additions.

For the longer haul, the prospects are more discouraging. As pointed

Table 6-1. Year-End Balances of Prior-Year Budget Authority, Fiscal Years 1980–93
Billions of current dollars

Year	Total	Obligated	Unobligated
1980	92.1	67.9	24.2
1981	112.8	86.3	26.5
1982	142.2	107.6	34.6
1983	172.1	128.7	43.4
1984	205.1	153.5	51.6
1985	244.3	182.9	61.5
1986	258.5	198.9	59.7
1987	260.1	212.5	47.6
1988	259.2	216.9	42.3
1989	251.0	211.1	39.9
1990	251.0	206.6	44.4
1991[a]	252.1	211.3	40.8
1992[a]	237.5	201.1	36.4
1993[a]	232.7	196.4	36.3

Source: Defense Budget Project, *Analysis of the FY 1992–93 Defense Budget Request* (Washington, February 7, 1991), table 5.
a. Estimated.

out in some detail by the Congressional Budget Office, the chances appear rather poor for reconciling next-generation weapons procurement with the proposed force structure and with budgets that are presumably to level off in real terms by fiscal 1997. Indeed, the CBO estimates that under the conditions of a no-growth budget and a constant force structure, another substantial gap will open between the funding required for these programs and the available resources.[6] Without remedial action, something will have to give—whether it is forces, readiness, programs, or level budgets.

Insurance

Still more discouraging is the high probability that, unless decisions about this issue are made now, the range of choice will become much smaller and more costly in the future. It is always tempting to put off such hard choices when the future is uncertain and final decisions about the allocation of resources lie some years ahead. Frequently, it is even good policy to defer final commitment on a decision until further data become available—at some cost.

There are several reasons, however, why deferral may prove more costly than the alternatives in this particular case. First, Desert Storm demonstrated in a way that no previous analyses could do the United States' wide margin of superiority over potential foes in weapons, training, and coordination. This was most evident in land-based airpower, which proved to be the dominant force in the war with Iraq. Second, there is more than one way to hedge against the uncertainties of the future and preserve that superiority. Third, not to adopt a long-range investment policy now is to lose flexibility of choice in the future.

Without a policy that clearly defines key points of decision, understood and respected by everyone involved, programs that begin at modest cost—at least by the standards of defense spending—can balloon into major consumers of resources and develop powerful constituencies for their continuation into procurement. Unless firm policies are established now, the waste and pain endured by Secretary Cheney in order to bring his budgets under control are likely to dog his successors in another six or seven years. When problems in the United States are large and resources for public purposes remain scarce, that is not a good way to conduct the business of defense.

Endnotes

1. J. M. and M. J. Cohen, *The Penguin Dictionary of Modern Quotations*, 2d ed. (Penguin Books, 1971), p. 165.

2. Jim Wolfe, "Cuba and North Korea Top the Chairman of the Joint Chiefs' List of World Villains," *Army Times*, April 15, 1991, p. 4.

3. Wolfe, "Cuba and North Korea."

4. Department of Defense, *1991 Joint Military Net Assessment* (March 1991), pp. 12–27.

5. Stephen S. Rosenfeld, "Gulf Giddiness," *Washington Post*, May 31, 1991, p. A19.

6. Statement of Robert E. Hale, assistant director, National Security Division, Congressional Budget Office, before the House Committee on Armed Services, March 19, 1991, pp. 22–26; and Fred Kaplan, "Guns Outpacing Butter," *Boston Globe*, March 20, 1991, p. 17.

CHAPTER SEVEN

THREE STANDARD OPTIONS

FORCE PLANNING is largely an exercise in coping with uncertainty. In part, the uncertainty arises from the difficulty of replicating combat conditions and events by means of war games or mathematical models, although the creation of national training centers by the services (led by the Air Force) had a significant payoff in the war against Iraq. To an equal if not greater extent, the uncertainty exists because of the growth in sophistication of non-nuclear as well as nuclear weapons.

Despite advances in the collection (if not the analysis) of intelligence, it has been possible to assess the capabilities of potential enemies only about two years into the future with a reasonable degree of confidence. And unless other nations become as transparent as the United States, it seems unlikely that analysts will be able to do much better in the coming decade. This means that uncertainty about foreign capabilities will grow exponentially beyond the two-year mark. Potential foes may not have decided how to allocate their resources after a limited period of time; that factor alone can account for some of the uncertainty. Also important is the simple reality that the development of new weapons can take much longer than several years. The disparity between what the opposition is deploying now and what it might deploy three or more years later is bound to create uncertainty. As a consequence, U.S. defense planners must make bets about the future and take out hedges against uncertainties, a problem familiar to stock market analysts and financial advisers.

Responses to Uncertainty

Obviously there are several types of solutions to the problem. In the recent past, the United States has for the most part followed a quite conservative policy despite periodic alarms about bomber and missile gaps, windows of vulnerability, and non-nuclear inferiority in Europe. It has maintained substantial nuclear and non-nuclear forces at a high level of readiness. At the same time, it was investing heavily in modernizing its arsenal of weapons as rapidly as budgets and technology permitted. In effect, U.S. leaders were betting that the Soviet Union was a near-term threat because of existing numerical advantages and that it would become a longer-term equal in technological sophistication. As a consequence, although nearly 60 percent of U.S. defense resources went to the operation and support of existing forces, more than 40 percent went into investment as late as 1990. Of total investment, 45 percent or more went to the development and production of next-generation equipment and the upgrading of the existing arsenal.

The Pentagon's Reaction

The administration's new FYDP is similarly conservative. There appears to be substantial agreement, at least outside the Pentagon, that the reduced forces planned for the mid-1990s will be fully sufficient to deal with another Iraq, even though no one other than General Powell seems to have identified who will replace Saddam Hussein as the designated villain. Despite the end of the cold war, Secretary Cheney gives every indication of being as enamored as his predecessors with the old era's investment policies. Admittedly, he has protected the operating and support budgets in his latest FYDP and attempted to streamline the Pentagon's process of weapons acquisition. Still, he demonstrates keen enthusiasm for such dubious next-generation programs as the B-2 stealth bomber, a modified version of the first-phase deployment of SDI, ground-based stealth missiles for the Army, stealth fighters for the Navy as well as the Air Force, and a hybrid C-17A for airlift. What is more, he is trying to cancel many of the systems currently in production in order to help pay for the next generation.

Several consequences flow from this decision. One is that some major production lines may grow cold well before they are retooled for the next generation. Another is that, as in the case of the B-2, production lines are started and aircraft begin to appear while proto-

types are still undergoing test and evaluation. This practice of concur-
rency is basically a relic of the cold war competition with the Soviet
Union, but it remains alive despite the lack of a major replacement for
the USSR. A third consequence is that the costs of these new systems
will end up being so high, as the CBO has noted, that even the budgets
proposed by Secretary Cheney will lack the funds to pay for all of
them without some sacrifice in such other areas as force structure or
readiness.

Finally, the fascination with high technology regardless of cost, and
the residual effects of the brief but exciting reign of the nuclear age,
endanger the funding for less glamorous but essential programs.
Strategic nuclear forces are bound to remain a key component of
defense, though much less important than in the past. Furthermore,
to the extent that these forces have deterred the USSR from undertaking
large-scale adventures, they should be able to exercise even greater
restraint on much smaller powers. Conceivably, modest ground-based
defenses that fit within the constraints of the ABM treaty would
strengthen the U.S. threat, but at a high price.

None of this need mean that the Pentagon should continue to lavish
resources on the strategic forces. Far more worthy of attention is the
military transportation system, for which the C-17 does very little on
the margin at very high cost. Airlift remains the Federal Express of
the system—indispensable for moving relatively small amounts of very
valuable cargo at high speed and high cost. The true heavy lifter has
been, is, and will remain sealift, which is slower but cheaper. The
Pentagon plans to improve military airlift with the replacement of the
C-141s by the C-17A and to expand sealift by 50 percent in order to
assure a faster overseas buildup. During Desert Shield, personnel and
light equipment moved rapidly to Saudi Arabia by air, while heavy
equipment arrived later by sea. The introduction of the C-17A will not
appreciably change the weight and speed of a comparable deployment
in the future. Moreover, according to the joint military net assessment,
even the proposed expansion of the transportation system as a whole
will support only one substantial buildup at a time. And that will remain
the case as long as the strategic concept, the forces, and the military
transportation system are not better balanced.

This defect and the Joint Staff's typically gloomy assessment of the
overall effectiveness of the programmed forces have not kept Secretary
Cheney from saying, "I am comfortable with the capabilities that these

forces will possess," and adding that, unless there is a reversal of the
Soviet military withdrawal from Germany and Poland, the smaller
U.S. forces will be "prudently matched to the threat we have been
projecting."[1] Indeed, a somewhat less pessimistic view of impending
threats might even lead to the conclusion that the programmed forces
could deal with a replay of the Iraqi contingency and still provide
substantial hedges against other, even less probable, threats to the key
conditions of U.S. security.

A Modest Proposal

It is from this perspective that the current FYDP can be considered
a high-cost, conservative response to the spectrum of future possible
dangers. If defense planners were to adopt a more realistic appraisal
of the international environment, they would be hard put not to come
to three general conclusions. First, they would recognize that the
future ability of the United States to maintain the conditions of its
security will depend as much on its moral authority, diplomatic skills,
and economic assets as on its military capabilities. Second, they would
accept the possibility of exchanging marginal military programs for
increased economic investment. Third, they would acknowledge that
in a less threatening environment they could design a more efficient
defense program than the FYDP proposes.

Such a program would accept, with some significant exceptions, the
Pentagon's reduced force structure and investment plan as an interim
goal to be reached by fiscal 1996. It would also abide by the ceilings
placed on national defense budget authority by the Budget Enforcement
Act for fiscal 1992 and 1993. Starting in fiscal 1994, however, it would
begin to reduce defense budget authority by an average of 6.5 percent
a year (in 1992 dollars) with the goal of reaching a budget of $169.2
billion (in 1992 dollars) by the year 2001 (see the "low option" in
table 7-1). Cumulatively, this would be lower than the Cheney FYDP
of $2.5 trillion by $316 billion in 1992 dollars. If it proves to be the
case that the Pentagon's defense program will require real increases
starting in fiscal 1997, as the CBO anticipates, the cumulative difference
between the low option and a larger alternative FYDP would amount
to more than $600 billion in constant dollars by 2001.

The low option would modify the assumptions underlying the

Table 7-1. Estimates of Cheney Future-Years Defense Programs and Low Option, Fiscal Years 1992–2001
Billions of 1992 dollars

Year	Cheney FYDP	Alternative Cheney FYDP[a]	Low option	Saving from Cheney FYDP	Saving from alternative FYDP
1992	278.3	278.3	278.3	0	0
1993	267.3	267.3	267.3	0	0
1994	257.8	257.8	246.0	11.8	11.8
1995	251.0	251.0	232.0	19.0	19.0
1996	243.7	243.7	225.2	18.5	18.5
1997	243.7	262.0	212.7	31.0	49.3
1998	243.7	281.6	200.9	42.8	80.7
1999	243.7	302.7	189.7	54.0	113.0
2000	243.7	325.3	179.2	64.5	146.1
2001	243.7	349.7	169.2	74.5	180.5
Total (051)	2,516.6	2,819.4	2,200.5	316.1	618.9

Sources: *Department of Defense Annual Report, Fiscal Year 1992*, p. 24; and authors' estimates.
a. Assumes that all next-generation weapons, including GPALS, are put into production and begin to be deployed.

Cheney proposals between 1992 and 1996 and depart from them during the next five years. At first, planners would agree that more time is needed to assess trends in the USSR, the Middle East, and the Korean peninsula before changing the Pentagon's expectations about contingencies in any substantial way. However, completion of the treaties on strategic arms reductions and cuts in non-nuclear forces from the Atlantic to the Urals should permit the United States to regard future Soviet nuclear and non-nuclear capabilities as less dangerous than assumed in the Cheney FYDP.

This change would permit the United States to stay literally as well as figuratively within the START ceiling on strategic nuclear forces of 6,000 warheads, propose that the USSR do likewise, and reduce the ICBM and bomber legs of the triad sufficiently to abide by the constraint. In addition, the non-nuclear forces allocated to the Atlantic command could be cut by at least two divisions and one carrier battle group as greater reliance is placed on land-based tactical airpower following the experience of Desert Storm.

Equally important, next-generation weapons designed to respond to a Soviet threat of cold war proportions would be held in the stage of advanced development, and more of them would be terminated than Secretary Cheney has recommended. In the strategic realm, this would mean giving up the B-1B's role as a penetrating bomber and reconfiguring it at lower cost to become a cruise missile launcher; terminating production of the B-2 at fifteen aircraft, but continuing its test and evaluation as a non-nuclear delivery system, as recommended by Representative Les Aspin;[2] deferring any decision to deploy the small ICBM but planning to place it in silos as a substitute for remaining MX and Minuteman III ICBMs in return for an agreement by the USSR to destroy its remaining 154 SS-18 ICBMs allowed by the START treaty; reorienting the strategic defense initiative to a research endeavor; and focusing development of active defenses on ground-based systems, both strategic and tactical.

For the non-nuclear forces, the acquisition policy would go beyond the changes proposed by Secretary Cheney and require continued upgrading of the current generation of combat aircraft and the deferral of production decisions on all next-generation successors; postponing a range of capabilities intended to multiply the Army's ability to contain a Soviet attack; extending the life of the C-141 airlift aircraft and terminating the C-17A; and canceling the SSN-21 attack submarine and any procurement funds for two new nuclear-powered aircraft carriers (CVN-76 and 77).

These changes, together with modest reductions in the Cheney force structure, would permit cumulative real savings in defense of $49.3 billion by the end of fiscal 1996 (table 7-1). Thereafter, it is estimated that the Cheney plan stabilizes the defense budget, in real terms, at the 1996 level on the assumption that the international environment remains about as it was in 1991.

The low option, by contrast, assumes that favorable international trends will have continued and that all the traditional demons either will have left the world stage or will be on the verge of disappearing. The Soviet Union, in this perspective, will establish a federal state, move toward more democratic institutions and a market economy, and shift to smaller armed forces based on voluntary service. Its leadership will continue to welcome arms reduction and express strong interest in lessening the burden of non-nuclear naval forces. Because of the verification regimes already in place, the Kremlin will offer to conclude informal agreements in a number of areas as a substitute for the tedious and time-consuming negotiations that have preceded formal treaties. No new Iraq (not even the old one) will emerge, but tensions will arise between Israel and the Arab states, and the sale of arms to creditworthy Arab states, with the exception of Iraq, will continue. Iran's leaders will remain preoccupied with strengthening its economy, and, despite a large oil income, will enter the arms market only selectively. In northeast Asia, China will not yet have engaged in a major modernization of its armed forces and, in any event, will be primarily concerned about its borders with the USSR, India, and southeast Asia. Kim Il Sung will have gone to his reward, and North Korea will redouble its efforts to establish economic ties with Japan and the United States. Whatever may have happened to Fidel Castro, Cuba will turn to the European community for aid to rebuild its collapsed economy.

The conditions of U.S. security would not change in these circumstances. But the forces for their maintenance would diminish considerably. Strategic nuclear forces would remain necessary, but the target list would shrink to fewer than 2,000 separate aiming points as the United States reduces the number of Soviet cities held at risk and the Soviets agree to dismantle their SS-18 ICBMs and cut back their non-nuclear capabilities. Furthermore, considering the improvement in Soviet-American relations and the hedge against surprise attack provided by the SLBMs aboard Trident submarines, the measure of performance (and of deterrence) becomes how well the strategic forces perform when, on a second strike, they launch from a generated alert (table 7-2).

The contingencies needed to determine the size and composition of the non-nuclear forces would become increasingly hard to imagine. Moreover, the probability of two simultaneous attacks on areas of critical interest to the United States would become even lower than in the past, when no such eventuality arose in forty-five years. Western Europe may still want a U.S. military presence after 1996, but it need not be a large one: perhaps a heavy Army active-duty division and two regular Air Force fighter wings. At this late date any chance that the Soviet Union would revert to type, adopt a bellicose posture, and rapidly deploy a large, high-quality offensive force is extremely remote. A slower reversal, of course, cannot be ruled out. But the U.S. contribution need not exceed a total of seven Army divisions and twelve fighter wings along with mine layers, surface combatants, attack submarines, and P-3 antisubmarine warfare (ASW) aircraft provided

Table 7-2. Low Option: Forces and Costs, Fiscal Year 2001
Billions of 1992 dollars

Type of force	Annual cost
Strategic nuclear forces	
41 B-1Bs	2.7
492 advanced cruise missiles	0.3
128 KC-135 tankers	1.7
198 National Guard air defense fighters	0.4
100 Minuteman III ICBMs	0.5
432 Trident D-5 SLBMs	11.7
Intelligence and communications	4.1
Ground-based ABM site	2.2
Tactical nuclear forces	0
Non-nuclear forces	
7 active Army divisions	21.4
4 reserve Army divisions	2.2
3 active Marine divisions/wings	13.9
1 reserve Marine division/wing	1.2
15 active Air Force fighter wings	30.7
11 reserve Air Force fighter wings	4.6
6 carrier battle groups (114 ships and submarines)	22.9
145 other battle force ships and submarines	13.4
260 P-3C ASW aircraft	2.7
820 airlift aircraft	10.9
255 sealift ships	2.5
National intelligence and communications	19.2
Total (051)	169.2

Source: Authors' estimates.

by the Navy (table 7-3). Such forces would be more than adequate to complement allied defenses, even if the Soviets were to dare to use whatever forces they would have kept deployed in the Far East.

Perhaps the worst, if not the most plausible, contingency that could arise in the Middle East in the late 1990s is a coalition of Arab states preparing for an all-out attack on Israel. Because of the lack of space in Israel itself, any U.S. support other than material assistance might have to come from sea-based forces. In fact, this is one of the few theaters in the world where the power-projection forces of the Navy— carrier battle groups and Marine amphibious forces—might be more than an expensive part of the scenery. After a preliminary bombardment of targets by ten B-2s and thirty B-52s, a Marine amphibious force of one division and its air wing, supported in a landing operation by three carrier battle groups, would seize a beachhead large enough to support another Marine division and its air wing (table 7-3). An assault of this magnitude should be enough to relieve pressure on the Israeli armed forces and threaten the enemies' line of retreat. Still another justification for the power-projection forces could come from a decision to strike hard at Libya, assuming Colonel Gadhafi is still in residence there. A total of four carrier battle groups (out of a fleet of six) could not only support a Marine landing, but also strike inland at other targets.

Any serious demand for U.S. forces in northeast Asia is almost certain to decline, as is the need to maintain significant U.S. deployments in Japan, Korea, and the Philippines. Still, as a hedge against a revived North Korean threat, supported once again by China, it might be prudent to retain a slimmer version of the current deployment in South Korea (one division and four Air Force fighter squadrons). These forces would be supported by a Marine division at Okinawa, with its air wing in Hawaii, and an active-duty Army division drawn from Hawaii, along with eleven Air Force fighter squadrons. Naval forces would consist of convoy escorts, nuclear attack submarines, and eighty-seven P-3 ASW aircraft.

In addition to these allocations, special operations forces, two divisions (one Army and one reserve Marine Corps), eight Air Force reserve wings, and all airlift and sealift, except for the C-130s, would be held in the continental United States. So would two carrier battle groups undergoing overhaul or training. The ground and tactical air forces, along with the special operations forces and one carrier battle group, could be made available either as reinforcements to one of the main theaters or as a Caribbean task force.

Some Comparisons

It is difficult to say whether the performance of the low option would approach that of the Cheney FYDP. If overseas presence is an important measure of adequacy (a dubious proposition), the FYDP would presumably station more land-based forces in Europe than the low option, but both would put about the same number in northeast Asia. The Navy would certainly argue that the Cheney option is the better of the two because, with twelve carrier battle groups, it could support four on station and surge a total of nine overseas in an emergency. The low option, by contrast, could maintain only two on

Table 7-3. Low Option: Allocation of Non-nuclear Forces, by Planning Contingency, Fiscal Year 2001

Force planning contingency	Army divisions		Marine divisions/ wings		Air Force wings		Carrier battle groups	Other			
	Active	Reserve	Active	Reserve	Active	Reserve		Ships	Aircraft	Airlift	Sealift
North Norway	...	...	...	...	...	...	...	...	...	...	...
Central Europe	3	4	...	...	9	3	...	...	...	...	...
Mediterranean	...	...	...	...	...	...	1	...	...	...	...
Atlantic	...	...	...	...	...	...	...	73	130	210	...
Middle East/Persian Gulf	...	...	2/2	...	...	...	3	...	...	...	...
Korea	2	...	1/1	...	5[a]	...	...	...	...	...	...
Pacific	...	...	...	...	...	...	...	72	130	210	...
Alaska	1	...	...	...	1	...	...	...	...	...	...
Continental United States	1	...	...	1/1	...	8	2	...	...	400	255
Total	7	4	3/3	1/1	15	11	6	145	260	820	255

Sources: Table 7-2; and authors' estimates.
a. Cost of B-52G aircraft is included; cost of B-2 is not.

Table 7-4. A Comparison of Deliverable Nuclear Weapons, Fiscal Year 2001

Option	Weapons inventory	Alert weapons	Alert, survivable weapons	Deliverable weapons[a]
Cheney FYDP				
944 small ICBMs	944	850	34	27
50 MXs	500	450	18	14
90 B-1Bs	2,160	648	648	518
75 B-2As	1,500	450	450	360
432 Tridents	3,456	2,246	2,246	1,797
Total	8,560	4,644	3,396	2,716
Low option				
100 Minuteman IIIs	300	270	11	9
90 B-1Bs	2,160	648	648	518
432 Tridents	3,456	2,246	2,246	1,716
Total	5,916	3,164	2,905	2,243

Source: Authors' estimates.
a. Cost per deliverable weapon is $13.5 million under the Cheney FYDP and $7.6 million under the low option.

station and have a capability to surge four. However, presence is more a way of justifying a particular force structure than a measure of performance.

A better yardstick in the case of the strategic nuclear forces is the probability that they could destroy their assigned targets on a second strike from a day-to-day or a generated alert, assuming that the target list would be the same for the two capabilities. By this measure, the Cheney proposal would have a higher overall probability of kill than the low option, though both would cause enormous damage. Moreover, if the USSR were the enemy, the United States would suffer the same amount of damage if the GPALS ABM system were deployed (as called for by Cheney) or if it were not (as in the low option). However, the low option—with fewer of the use-them-or-lose-them ICBMs and bombers—would have a higher probability of halting the exchange before irreparable damage had been done to either side. As a consequence, to the extent that deterrence can be linked to hypothetical performance, the low option might well be the more effective of the two. The Cheney proposal might be the more powerful deterrent to more primitive nuclear powers, but the low option should also prove terrifying, even if those powers had deployed a few easily targetable, long-range delivery systems by the turn of the century (table 7-4).

Because the tactical nuclear forces of both the United States and

Table 7-5. The Test of Desert Storm

Type of force	Forces committed to Desert Storm	Forces available	
		Cheney proposal	Low option
Army divisions	8	18	11
Marine Corps brigades	6	11	11
Air Force fighter wings	10	26	26
Carrier battle groups	6	12	6

Sources: Walter S. Mossberg, "Even the Scaled-Down Military Machine Planned for '95 Would Leave the U.S. a Still-Potent Power," *Wall Street Journal*, March 14, 1991, p. A20; and authors' estimates.

the USSR are likely to have disappeared by the year 2001, whichever option is chosen, the performance of these capabilities would not be an issue. More important, in any event, is the adequacy of the two countries' non-nuclear forces to meet the dangers of the future. No clear answer to this question exists, despite the larger assets provided by the Cheney proposal. The outside world could be more or less treacherous than either option has estimated. The Cheney FYDP may have reached the point of diminishing returns to scale and may represent an overinvestment in these capabilities. The low option may not be high enough on the upward side of the performance curve, assuming agreement on how to draw the curve.

Nonetheless, a crude and conservative measure of adequacy, if not performance, has emerged from congressional hearings and debates on the defense budget. It is whether a given non-nuclear capability can generate the forces necessary to replicate Desert Storm. The measure is primitive for two main reasons. First, it is by no means evident that a genuine threat of the alleged magnitude of an Iraq led by another Saddam Hussein is likely to emerge during the coming ten years. Second, even though postmortems on Desert Storm have yet to be completed, it may well be the case that the United States committed larger forces to the campaign than were necessary to achieve the same outcome. Still, the Desert Storm criterion, on which some agreement exists, is better than nothing at all or hot disputes over models, measures, and the influence of alleged intangibles.

By this test, the Cheney proposal not only can reproduce the actual U.S. deployments for Desert Storm; it also retains forces for rotation, reinforcement, or other contingencies that might arise during such a campaign (table 7-5). However, it might well be short of the transportation necessary to deal with a simultaneous attack elsewhere, and some of its reserve forces would not yet be ready for combat. The low option would also provide the U.S. resources used by Desert Storm with one exception: at best, it could deploy only four ready carrier battle groups rather than the six used in Desert Storm. Moreover, the Contingency command (or possibly the Atlantic command; the jurisdictions of the two seem to overlap) would have to deploy all but one of the active-duty divisions and most of the regular land-based fighter wings to this one theater. The enlarged transportation command would presumably be somewhat less severely tested than it was in actuality, even without the C-17A. But it would have little remaining lift capacity to move forces elsewhere. The importance of the shortage, however, would be minimal. There would remain mostly reserve forces to move—and the ground components would not yet have achieved an acceptable level of combat readiness by the time any mobility forces would have become available. Still, the low option could meet the test of Desert Storm and do so at roughly 70 percent of the cost of the Cheney proposal. Admittedly, it would hedge much less against other simultaneous contingencies. But the price of such insurance is high and the probability that the coverage would be needed is very low.

An Intermediate Option

These assessments do not mean that only two options are open to policymakers. They simply represent, realistically, the two ends of what is seen as the current range of choices. A third type of option might consist of parts taken from the other two. Such an option might choose the low option's strategic nuclear and naval forces and its modernization policy. However, it might move somewhat closer to the Cheney proposal with respect to ground forces and actually go beyond it in the retention of Air Force fighter wings. The rationale for this mix of capabilities would draw heavily on the strategic concept of the low option, but the larger active-duty ground and tactical air forces would make it easier to meet the goals of another Desert Storm. Additional regular ground and fighter units would also allow for rotation, reinforcement, and another small contingency. And the greater emphasis on land-based fighter wings would reflect the dominance of the Air Force in the campaign to free Kuwait.

The annual budget authority for this intermediate type of option

Table 7-6. Intermediate Option: Forces and Costs, Fiscal Year 2001
Billions of 1992 dollars

Type of force	Annual cost
Strategic nuclear forces	
45 B-1Bs	3.0
1,080 advanced cruise missiles	0.7
135 KC-135 tankers	1.8
198 National Guard air defense fighters	0.4
100 Minuteman III ICBMs	0.5
432 Trident D-5 SLBMs	11.7
Intelligence and communications	4.1
Ground-based ABM site	2.3
Nuclear interdiction weapons	1.5
Non-nuclear forces	
9 active Army divisions	27.5
6 reserve Army divisions	3.3
3 active Marine divisions/wings	15.6
1 reserve Marine division/wing	1.2
18 active Air Force fighter wings	36.8
13 reserve Air Force fighter wings	5.4
9 carrier battle groups (171 ships and submarines)	34.4
175 other battle forces ships and submarines	16.2
260 P-3C ASW aircraft	2.7
820 airlift aircraft	10.9
255 sealift ships	2.5
National intelligence and communications	19.2
Total (051)	201.7

Source: Authors' estimates.

would amount to $201.7 billion (in 1992 dollars) by fiscal 2001 (table 7-6). With the Cheney proposal as the baseline, the cumulative real saving from following a compromise course would amount to $209 billion over the ten-year period. As usual, the premium for the additional insurance would be high.

Choices

To put forward the Cheney proposal and two other options may be seen as the avoidance of choice (table 7-7). It can also be argued that the time has not yet come to make decisions about the defense of the United States and its interests for the next ten years. To wait, and in fact to follow the path laid out by the secretary of defense, is to buy

Table 7-7. Three Budgets for the Annual Cost of Force Planning Contingencies, Fiscal
Years 1996 and 2001
Billions of 1992 dollars

Force planning contingency	Cheney (1996)	Intermediate option (2001)	Low option (2001)
Strategic nuclear deterrence	41.8	24.5	23.6
Tactical nuclear deterrence	1.5	1.5	. . .
Non-nuclear defense of:			
North Norway	12.2	1.2	. . .
Central Europe	44.0	32.8	31.1
Mediterranean	7.6	3.8	3.8
Atlantic sea lanes	21.7	12.9	4.8
Middle East/Persian Gulf	55.1	45.0	29.0
South Korea	17.3	22.4	20.9
Pacific sea lanes	14.7	12.9	4.8
Alaska	1.0	5.1	5.1
Panama and Caribbean	3.2	. . .	. . .
Continental United States	4.4	20.4	26.9
National intelligence and communications	19.2	19.2	19.2
Total (051)	243.7	201.7	169.2

Sources: Table 5-6; and authors' estimates.

the time to reduce uncertainty about the future strength of current international trends. Indeed, both positions have much to be said for them.

Unfortunately, however, there is a dilemma here. On the one hand, the president and his principal advisers certainly deserve to have a range of choices, including the option to defer setting longer-range goals. On the other hand, defense is a business of making decisions with long-range implications, of weighing the costs, benefits, and risks that will result from each major choice. Even if a decision were made today to start producing the Air Force F-22 stealth fighter once test and evaluation has been completed, operational models probably would not begin to make their way into the tactical inventory until the last years of the century. During that period the Soviets could conceivably produce highly effective and relatively cheap countermeasures to the aircraft. But there is also a nontrivial probability that the Soviets' ability to compete in this complex area of technology will have collapsed and that an upgraded F-15E could remain the dominant and much cheaper fighter well into the twenty-first century.

In such circumstances, buying time through a carefully phased investment strategy obviously makes sense. Even in the acquisition process, however, and certainly in the determination of force size and composition, there is much to be said for having long-range (but adjustable) goals and a sense of key points of choice along the way to reaching them. They help the president to consider whether resources will become available for other purposes or whether he must plan on setting aside additional funds for defense and decide which pockets will be deep enough to provide them. They also assist defense policymakers to act systematically on the broad range of choices put before them—there are always more claims than funds—and recognize in advance where critical decisions will have to be made. Most important of all, knowledge of the goals helps the entire national security community to concentrate on creating the conditions favorable to their attainment. For example, maintaining constraints on Iraq would obviously help the process.

The changes in the Soviet Union and the advances demonstrated in Desert Storm, particularly in air power, are remarkable. Yet none of the three options reviewed thus far assumes that international politics will undergo a major transformation. That could be a valid assumption. However, there is a significant probability that the opportunity now exists for a more advanced system of cooperative security and for a U.S. defense budget still more constrained than the lowest option considered so far.

Endnotes

1. *Department of Defense Annual Report, Fiscal Year 1992*, pp. v, 3, 7.
2. Representative Les Aspin, chairman, House Committee on Armed Services, "The B-2 Stealth Bomber: How Many and for What?" speech before the Electronic Industries Association, Washington, June 11, 1991.

CHAPTER EIGHT

THE COOPERATIVE SECURITY OPTION

ALTHOUGH THE Pentagon's future-years defense program acknowledges the diminished possibility of a large-scale threat emerging from the Soviet Union on short notice, it nonetheless preserves the traditional commitment to react rapidly to unanticipated acts of aggression anywhere in the world. This capability is to be provided primarily by U.S. forces, acting unilaterally if necessary. It is presumed that residual commitments in Europe will continue to be supported by traditional NATO allies and similar arrangements will be preserved in Japan and Korea. Alliance arrangements are less clearly specified, however, in other areas of the world, which are now perceived as more likely sources of conflict. The plan assumes therefore that U.S. forces might have to mount a major military operation with no more than a few weeks' warning while simultaneously preserving their capabilities in other sensitive areas.

The experience of the Persian Gulf war strengthened these assumptions, as well as confidence in the ability of U.S. forces to meet their requirements. The original Iraqi attack on Kuwait was a major surprise, indicating yet again that anticipation and preventive action cannot be relied upon. Moreover, the international response, clearly initiated and coordinated by the United States, was decisively effective. In particular, the United States displayed a capacity for precise tactical air operations that for now is unique in the world. It would not be easy to duplicate the combination of functions on which such operations are based: the rapid gathering, processing, and dissemination of necessary information; the immediate translation of that information into operational plans; and the effective implementation of those plans by people and equipment. It would probably require a decade or more for a major competitor to arise, because all of the world's other military establishments are deficient in one or more of the principal ingredients.

It is therefore natural and politically attractive for the United States to rest its security posture on this laboriously developed comparative advantage. Precise tactical air operations do appear to be decisive against any substantial ground force invasion that potential aggressors might attempt. If ground forces can no longer be used to seize and hold territory, then the scope of likely threat is reduced to long-range bombardment, guerrilla warfare, and terrorist actions. Diminished tensions between the major powers have sharply reduced the international political leverage of these latter two forms of violence. In any event, the former is more suited to retribution than to any politically useful initiative.

It is not prudent to assume, however, that the recently displayed comparative advantage in tactical air operations can be preserved indefinitely against dedicated efforts to match or negate it. The core technology on which it is based is widely dispersed in international commercial markets, and it is those markets, rather than military programs, that are driving fundamental technical development. Although the military application of this technology is time-consuming and difficult, fundamental access to it cannot be denied. Moreover, currently underdeveloped military organizations that are not encumbered by traditional weapons design and procurement practices might learn to be more efficient in adopting commercially available technology. If U.S. security policy serves to make the development of advanced conventional munitions the focus of international competition, significant competitors might arise at a surprising rate.

For these reasons it is also not prudent to ignore the opportunity to create an international security arrangement that is inherently more efficient than unregulated national competition. The Soviet military establishment, still the major source of potentially threatening military capability, is clearly attempting to escape the unmanageable burdens of sustaining confrontation against all the other industrial economies. If the Soviet establishment would systematically and constructively join in the management of military deployments, all countries could achieve better security at substantially lower cost.

The key to that efficiency is reduced uncertainty. Systematic regulation of military deployments would mean that dangerous offensive threats could not be organized without lengthy preparations and unambiguous violations of the arrangements. Large sums can be saved if the necessary response time of military forces is reliably lengthened. In addition, systematic regulation involving all the major military establishments offers the best chance, perhaps the only realistic one, of controlling the general proliferation of advanced weapons—the most predictable long-term source of threat.

Given these background conditions, it is not responsible for U.S. military planners to rely indefinitely on the traditional assumptions that underlie the current FYDP, attractive as that might seem to those who produce and operate advanced conventional weapons and are justifiably proud of their accomplishments. U.S. interests would be better served by a general cooperative security arrangement. Rather than attempting to sustain unilateral military advantage, it is imperative to transform it into reliable means of cooperation.

This process would involve a meaningful shift in the assumptions used to guide investment in U.S. forces. Rather than preparing to respond to unanticipated acts of aggression and to do so unilaterally if necessary, U.S. forces would be designed to prevent aggressive actions from being organized in the first place. They would operate in direct cooperation with the other military establishments to define and enforce the necessary operational rules. U.S. forces would retain their military capabilities until a satisfactory arrangement had been created, and would preserve them in lesser amounts thereafter as a guarantor of the arrangement's integrity. To achieve the stability and efficiency of cooperation, however, U.S. forces would have to be subjected to international regulations.

In order to define such an arrangement and to pursue it seriously, U.S. military planning would have to broaden its scope considerably. This would require supplementing the current focus on weapons projects and traditional military missions with a concern for the principles and methods of cooperative regulation. With regard to a reconstituted Soviet government in particular, the U.S. military would have to subordinate traditional objectives of deterrence and containment to the strategic principle of cooperative engagement that was successfully used with the German and Japanese military establishments following World War II. Such a substantial transformation of policy is internally very difficult, of course, and is rarely accomplished by large, well-developed organizations. International events mandate a serious effort to make this transformation, however, and are likely to compel the United States to debate it as a viable security option.

Basic Design

The underlying premise of a cooperative security arrangement is that the participating military organizations are all on the same side, are all defensively configured, and are all primarily committed to providing mutual reassurance. This requires them to systematically limit offensive capabilities that might support ground invasions or might undertake long-range bombardment to achieve some political objective.

In order to make these assumptions of cooperation more than a polite form of traditional deterrence and containment, they would have to be embodied in a series of adjustments in the size, mission commitments, and operational practices of deployed forces. A fully developed arrangement would involve all of the following provisions.

—*Normalized aggregate firepower*. To inhibit the ability to assemble superior concentration of ground forces along a potential axis of attack, a standard ground force unit would be defined in terms of manpower and equipment, and ceilings would be set on the number of such units each military establishment could have. The number of units allowed would be normalized in terms of the extent of national territory to be defended so that all countries follow a common standard of density (amount of force for a given amount of ground area) low enough to signal defensive rather than offensive intent.

—*Controlled concentration and movement*. Because a common density standard would not preclude localized offensive concentrations, the normal locations of ground force units would also be defined, and movements away from these locations would be constrained by rate (number of units allowed to move in a given amount of time) and by rules of prior announcement.

—*Management of tactical air assets*. Because even defensively configured ground force operations can be severely degraded by precise tactical air attack, and the success of such attacks is highly sensitive to initiation and surprise, the composition of tactical air deployments would be regulated to favor defense over deep interdiction. Moreover, the routine management of military air traffic would be internationalized in sensitive areas.

—*Transparency*. To protect the arrangement from any rapid, unanticipated, nationally initiated change, rules of disclosure would be imposed on basic research activities, new weapons deployment plans, and major operational exercises. These provisions would necessarily allow some degree of national security classification, but that would be limited to technical and operational detail. Fundamental purposes and basic time schedules would have to be revealed in advance.

—*Residual nuclear forces*. Because nuclear weapons, even in small numbers, are extremely dangerous to conventional force configurations and to industrial societies, it is difficult to make them compatible with the general principle of defensive force configurations. It is possible to imagine their removal either by direct agreement or by highly effective defenses. However, either method would require a degree of cooperation extending in detail, intrusiveness, and reliable effectiveness well beyond the other provisions of the cooperative security arrangement. A more practical and commensurate arrangement for nuclear weapons would therefore involve some compromise: offensive forces would be retained at significantly reduced levels, but their technical configuration and operational practices would be made much more strictly retaliatory than they currently are.

—*Consolidated weapons export controls*. To ensure that the cooperative arrangement is not undermined by outside military establishments, integrated controls would be imposed on weapons exports and directly related technology. This would involve the common licensing of all weapons transfers to be sure they are consistent with the other regulations. It would also involve enforced end-use disclosure for all related technology trade and continuous monitoring designed to detect any patterns of diversion.

If the assumptions of cooperative security were actually adopted and the necessary regulations systematically implemented by the major military establishments—the United States, USSR, United Kingdom, France, Germany, Japan, and China, for example—they could legitimately be extended as a global security standard. It could be made very difficult in practical terms for any other country to flout them. The reductions in the major powers' force levels and the restrictions on their offensive capability would be an undeniable benefit to all other military forces. Compliance with the rules could justifiably be demanded as a price for that benefit. For those inclined to enjoy the benefit without paying the price, the consolidated weapons export controls would impose much more robust restrictions than currently exist. It is one thing to elude controls that are separately organized for different weapons categories, incompletely developed in all categories, and burdened by extensive secrecy and strong national competition among the major suppliers. It is quite another to do so if the major suppliers are explicitly cooperating, are enforcing disclosure, and are serious about imposing restrictions. Moreover, with an internationally legitimized, highly inclusive security arrangement in place, compliance could readily be made a condition for access to international financial markets. That would be a much stronger incentive than any yet attempted.

The major military establishments have not entirely forsaken the practice of confrontation and the residual psychology associated with it, and these lingering attitudes do impose significant barriers to cooperation. However, there does not appear to be any fundamental conflict in national political objectives sustaining these historical suspicions and antagonisms. That latter fact opens up the opportunity to pursue a cooperative security arrangement. Predictable interest in it among traditional U.S. allies, Germany in particular, adds a political catalyst to the substantial material incentives to develop the option.

Force Structure Implications

The basic principles and implementation of cooperative security do not yield an exact determination of the appropriate size of U.S. military forces. Judgments about that would undoubtedly be affected by the completeness and robustness of the arrangements. Nonetheless, it is apparent that a well-developed design of cooperative security would allow overall force deployments to be reduced even more than the levels called for in the lowest of the traditional options and would enable a substantial redesign of their composition. An outcome that might be achieved in a ten-year period is presented in table 8-1. The major elements of U.S. forces would all be less than half their current size in this projected outcome, but modernization would occur at a stable rate of replacement and operational training would maintain current standards. By 2001, the annual defense budget would be

Table 8-1. Cooperative Security Arrangement: Forces and Costs, Fiscal Year 2001
Billions of 1992 dollars

Item	Annual cost
Strategic nuclear forces	
100 Minuteman III ICBMs	0.6
40 B-1Bs	2.6
800 advanced cruise missiles	0.4
120 KC-135 tankers	1.3
36 F-15s (Air National Guard)	0.1
162 F-16s (Air Force Reserve)	0.3
240 Trident/C-4 SLBMs[a]	4.6
Intelligence and communications	3.8
Strategic defense initiative	1.0
Tactical nuclear forces	0
Non-nuclear forces	
Land	
7 active Army divisions	21.4
4 reserve Army divisions	2.2
3 active Marine divisions	5.9
1 reserve Marine division	0.6
Tactical air	
3 active Marine air wings	8.0
1 reserve Marine air wing	0.6
10 active Air Force fighter wings	20.5
7 reserve Air Force fighter wings	2.9
Naval	
6 carrier battle groups (114 ships)	22.9
2 brigades of amphibious lift (41 ships)	5.5
1-ocean ASW capability (76 ships)	10.6
Airlift and sealift	
70 C-5As	3.1
40 C-5Bs	1.7
234 C-141s	3.1
57 KC-10s	1.1
450 C-130s	2.0
8 SL-7s	0.3
32 cargo ships	0.5
28 tankers	0.5
15 other ships	1.1
National intelligence and communications	17.6
Total (051)	146.8

a. In order to meet the constraint of 3,000 total warheads, it is assumed that 90 of the 1,920 warhead slots would be held empty under the downloading rules of the treaty.

Table 8-2. Estimated Cooperative Security Budgets, Fiscal Years 1992–2001
Billions of 1992 dollars

Year	Cooperative security budget authority	Cheney FYDP	Low option	Saving from Cheney FYDP	Saving from low option
1992	278.3	278.3	278.3	0	0
1993	267.3	267.3	267.3	0	0
1994	246.0	257.8	246.0	11.8	0
1995	230.1	251.0	232.0	20.9	1.9
1996	213.5	243.7	225.2	30.2	11.7
1997	198.1	243.7	212.7	45.6	14.6
1998	183.8	243.7	200.9	59.9	17.1
1999	170.5	243.7	189.7	73.2	19.2
2000	158.2	243.7	179.2	85.5	21.0
2001	146.8	243.7	169.2	96.9	22.4
Total (051)	2,092.6	2,516.6	2,200.5	424.0	107.9

Sources: Table 7-1; and authors' estimates.

$146.8 billion in budget authority, about 50 percent of the current level. For the entire period, the cumulative total would be $424 billion less than Secretary Cheney's official FYDP and $107.9 billion less than the low traditional option (table 8-2).

Under this outcome, the Army would retain seven active divisions and the Marine Corps would retain three. That force would be capable of coordinating an operation of the size that was undertaken in the Persian Gulf but would be much less likely to encounter the need to do so. Five reserve divisions (four Army, one Marine) would protect against a major failure of the cooperative arrangement, allowing a fifteen-division force to be assembled if necessary in the course of about three months. With requirements for extensive disclosure in effect, a fifteen-division potential force would provide an ample base and adequate time for responding to a collapse of the arrangement and a renewal of a confrontational arms race.

Tactical air units under the illustrative force structure would be reduced from forty-four active and sixteen reserve air wings to a level of twenty-two active wings and nine reserves.[1] Since the reserve air wings are generally capable and available, thirty-one total air wings would be ready for service on short notice. With investment focused on the various technologies involved in defense evasion and precision delivery, the basic potential of these reduced forces would be at least comparable to the current larger forces at any given locus of engagement and would offer a much greater margin of safety against reduced levels of threat worldwide.

The illustrative force structure provides a total of 3,000 nuclear weapons, roughly one-third of the strategic nuclear weapons inventories expected to be maintained under prevailing arms control arrangements (including the recently concluded START treaty). The destructive capacity provided by nuclear forces of this reduced size would be ample to perform legitimate deterrent missions. This formulation allows a retaliatory threat to basic military and industrial assets but is meant to preclude, to the extent feasible, effective attack on opposing strategic weapons launchers—a target category that is currently the top priority of both the U.S. and the Soviet military establishments. In order to constrain forces designed for this mutually destabilizing priority, their composition would be adjusted to limit the multiple warhead systems that have been optimized for attack on opposing strategic launcher positions. Such attacks would have to be preemptive to justify the allocation of high-quality strategic assets, and that would violate the core principle of retaliation.

Because strategic forces with 3,000 warheads would have the inherent capability to perform tactical missions if necessary, and the plausible requirement for such missions dramatically recedes under a cooperative arrangement, all tactical nuclear weapons have been eliminated under the illustrative force structure. In addition to providing an obvious improvement in efficiency—the removal of redundant capacity—this would also improve the inherent safety of nuclear weapons operations, a matter likely to be a high-priority objective as the source of confrontation dissolves. The traditional engagement of tactical nuclear weapons in conventional force operations is clearly undesirable from the perspective of managerial safety.

The common theme that underlies the proposed reduction and reallocation of forces is a fundamentally different attitude toward uncertainty. By accepting restraint, this posture imposes restraint on all potential sources of threat. Rather than treating threat contingencies as if they were determined by uncontrollable and undetectable processes of nature, a cooperative security arrangement uses political leverage to organize constraints on uncertainty. That is undeniably a more intelligent approach to uncertainty, and responsible security policy must attempt to develop it.

This approach, moreover, becomes all the more compelling as the Soviet military establishment is caught up in the process of reconstituting a radically altered form of government. Whatever the eventual political outcome proves to be, the destructive potential of Soviet forces will remain substantial for the indefinite future. It is obviously inappropriate to confront them as potential aggressors and unwise to risk triggering a backlash of desperation by appearing to pursue Western military advantage. The new security imperative is to engage the Soviet establishment in international collaboration so as to overcome their isolation, to fashion constructive forms of influence, and to protect against a dangerous siege mentality. The exercise of creating a cooperative security arrangement is a natural means of accomplishing this purpose.

Endnote

1. The Marine Corps air component is currently organized in three active and one reserve air wings; these would be preserved under the illustrative force structure. Since they are roughly twice the size of the Air Force tactical air wings, they have been counted as two in this listing in order to make the unit of account comparable.

METHODOLOGY

THE FOLLOWING assumptions are the basis for the cost estimates in this book.

The annual cost of a U.S. weapon system or force package (such as a division) consists of the sum of its annualized investment and operating and support costs. The investment account encompasses three standard budgetary categories: procurement, RDT&E, and military construction. Operating and support costs are intended to capture military personnel, operation and maintenance, military family housing, and revolving and management funds.

Annual investment and operating and support costs reflect the indirect as well as the direct funding of defense capabilities. These costs are functions of the current replacement cost of a given weapon system or force package. As an example, a U.S. armored division has a current replacement value of $7 billion. Its investment coefficient is 0.1333, and its operating and support coefficient is 0.333. These and other coefficients, dealing with missiles, aircraft, and combat vehicles, ships, and submarines, are based on average historical correlations between replacement costs and the investment and operating and support costs.

The replacement cost of a weapon system or force package is a function of four factors: its original cost, the cost of subsequent modifications and improvements, inflation since its original acquisition, and the estimated annual cost of replacing it over a period of years that reflects the life cycle of the weapons and equipment. The $7 billion for an armored division indicates what it would cost to purchase the division (but not its personnel) in fiscal year 1992. If the life cycle of the division is fifteen years, and the next generation of its weapons and equipment is expected to cost twice their current price in real terms, the replacement cost would have to be raised each year by approximately 1.0473 ($2^{1/15}$). This annual increase would reflect the process of upgrades, RDT&E, and eventual procurement. It would also cause investment and operating and support costs to rise commensurately. By the fifteenth year, the replacement value would have doubled in real terms. So would the investment and operating and support costs. The design of a cost-oriented investment strategy is one way to control these increases.

The Office of the Assistant Secretary of Defense, Systems Analysis, developed much of this methodology in the 1960s and early 1970s. The *1991 Joint Military Net Assessment* contains calculations that appear to be based on a similar methodology.

Further information about the estimates in this book can be obtained from the Foreign Studies program of the Brookings Institution.